Real Estate Investing For Beginners

Make Passive Income with the Latest
Rental Property Investing , Wholesaling,
Development, Flipping Houses and
Marketing Strategies

Tony Toson

The following book is reproduced below with the goal of providing information that is as accurate and reliable as possible. Regardless, purchasing this book can be seen as consent to the fact that both the publisher and the author of this book are in no way experts on the topics discussed within and that any recommendations or suggestions that are made herein are for entertainment purposes only. Professionals should be consulted as needed prior to undertaking any of the action endorsed herein.

This declaration is deemed fair and valid by both the American Bar Association and the Committee of Publishers Association and is legally binding throughout the United States.

Furthermore, the transmission, duplication, or reproduction of any of the following work including specific information will be considered an illegal act irrespective of if it is done electronically or in print. This extends to creating a secondary or tertiary copy of the work or a recorded copy and is only allowed with express written consent from the Publisher. All additional rights reserved.

The information in the following pages is broadly considered to be a truthful and accurate account of facts—as such, any inattention, use, or misuse of the information in question by the reader will render any resulting actions solely under their purview. There are no scenarios in which the publisher or the original author of this work can be in any fashion deemed liable for any hardship or damages that may befall them after undertaking information described herein.

Additionally, the information in the following pages is intended only for informational purposes and should thus be thought of as universal. As befitting its nature, it is presented without assurance regarding its prolonged validity or interim quality. Trademarks that are mentioned are done without written consent and can in no way be considered an endorsement from the trademark holder.

Table of Contents

Introduction

We have all wanted to get into the real estate business because we wanted to acquire property or heard that people made big bucks and wanted a piece of the action. Sadly, not all people get out of the business with the same narrative. Many people lose their money or end up buying overpriced property that ties them down in debt.

The problem here is that most of us do not go in with any knowledge—we watch a YouTube video or listen to some folk talking, and we think that we are ready to sink into the business, bringing with us all the hard-earned money we have collected over the years. However, just as a doctor requires years of education and training to do a surgery on you, you also need organized knowledge to let you in on what you need to know about real estate investing.

This book is the ideal source of introductory information to guide you as you start dipping your toes in the business. When you go in prepared, real estate is bound to become your long-term business and a source of financial security and freedom.

To that end, the following chapter will provide an informative introduction to help beginners understand all the terms and concepts of real estate like rental property investing, REIT investing, flipping houses, wholesale real estate, and commercial trade estate. You will also learn about different types of real estate and how you can make passive income trading with them. You will also find a systematic guide on how you can turn this hustle into a long-term business, among other things.

Chapter 1: Real Estate Investing for Beginners

Investing in real estate is another method of putting your money to work today and allowing it to grow and multiply as time goes. For the investment to be worthwhile, though, the 'returns' or the 'profits' you get from your investment must be able to cover the taxes imposed on the property, the maintenance cost, insurance, the risks taken, and the costs of other utilities.

The concept of investing in real estate is quite simple. First, it requires a basic understanding of the nature of the investments economics involved and the risks you will be bear when you invest. To make a profit,

9

you must invest in properties, collect rent, and manage the money you get so that you can invest it in other businesses as well. Note that 'simple' does not mean that the real estate business is 'easy.' It is marred with risks—ranging from minor to large disasters that could make you lose your property or even worse.

Although there are risks involved, real estate investment remains one of the most popular and most lucrative investment ventures because of its straightforward approach. The business comprises a fair exchange between a property owner and the property user. As long as the user pays rent and as long and as long as the owner ensures that his property remains safe and with a proper connection (electricity and water, although the renter pays the bills), the deal is sealed. However, there may be added complexities depending on the type of real estate investments such as commercial, industrial, residential, and the kind that trades on stock exchanges called REITs.

Ways That Real Estate Investors Make Money

There are four ways to make money on the real estate vehicle:

Cash Flow Income

This is the kind of real estate investment where a

person purchases or constructs an apartment building and starts collecting rent from renters, thereby creating a stream of income in the form of rent. Rent is the amount of money that a tenant pays to a landlord to use their property for a specified period, usually, a month. Examples of spaces to rent include office buildings, car washes, some storage units, rental houses and apartments, and others.

Appreciation of Value

When the value of real estate property goes up due to changes in the market, it creates profits for the owners. For example, suppose a large mall is built next to your land, your land will become busier and scarcer because more people will be wanting to use it to create businesses that support the mall such as running a parking lot. Anything you construct there, such as apartment buildings, will be more attractive to renters and buyers than it could have been if the facility was not there.

Supplementary Investment Income

Real estate investing is an excellent source of supplementary income that comes from facilities like the laundry facilities installed in the low-income apartments and vending machines erected in office buildings. Facilities like these are similar to mini-businesses, and they help to supplement your income by providing services and products that your collection of customers will need.

Real Estate-Related Income

This is the income enjoyed by the real estate 'specialists,' the brokers, who make money through the commissions they receive when people sell or buy real estate property. There are also real estate management agencies employed to collect rent from tenants. Companies like those earn money by charging a commission for the rental income received. For example, a real estate company is hired to manage the daily operations in a hotel. The company might be allowed to take 5 percent of all sales, in exchange for running day-to-day operations like running the receptionist desk, hiring maids, washing the towels and mowing lawns.

The reality is that the majority of us will not get rich and attain financial independence by merely doing our jobs. One of the reasons is that the time we dedicate to work each day is not enough to achieve any tangible success. The much that many can do is feed, clothe and shelter themselves. They will afford luxuries like cars and vacations, but these will require them to bend their backs every day working.

For us to be financially independent, we need to come up with multiple streams of passive income. Passive income is income that you earn without needing to be physically present. Smart real estate investment is one of the ways to do this, for big returns with relatively low risks.

Investing in real estate can appear challenging although it is not. You only need to wrap your mind around some important basics before you dip your foot.

Real Estate Investment Types

Rental Property Investing

The most popular and common form of real estate investing is residential real estate. It includes investing in condos, single-family houses, and townhouses. These houses are built to be rented out or sold at a profit. For example, as an investor, you can buy a condo that is near the beach at $100,000 then rent it out on Airbnb for $100, and you will make a lot of money from it.

Large residential properties are those that are intended for use by businesses, and they often are categorized as commercial real estate. Owners of buildings like these make money from renting out office space or from renting out multi-family residential units. There is a rule that indicates that residential buildings that have more than 4 units should be classified as commercial buildings. A commercial-residential house will follow different lending criteria when it comes to the mortgage terms and conditions.

When trying to identify a good rental property, there are many factors you need to keep in mind. The first is that you will want to limit your search to neighborhoods that have low crime rates, well-rated schools, strong employment figures and those whose value is appreciating.

Once you have narrowed down your search to a particular area or specific properties, you should then run some calculations to see the prospects of those properties generating some income for you. The goal here is to find a property that will bring in a positive cash flow such that the rental income you earn is higher than the expenses you incur. It should cover the repairs, insurance, mortgage payments, property taxes, and management fees.

Another way to do this is to take up the 1% rule. This rule is used to determine whether some property is viable for investing in or not. Applying this rule, you took the estimated monthly rental income and divided it by the purchase price. If the figure you get is 1% or ranges just about there, then you can be sure that you have an excellent rental property.

For example, let's say you intend to purchase a property at $400,000 and you estimate the monthly income to be $4500 (assuming that there will be no vacant houses). Then using the 1% rule, divide the $4500 by $400,000 and you will get 1.13%, which should tell you that the property would be a viable investment.

One of the challenges of investing in rental property is the number of expenses involved. Before committing yourself to them, make a list of all possible costs. If you fail to include even one expense upfront, you will have an inaccurate estimate of the costs and consequently, of the income you expect.

The list of expenses is long, and it includes things like broker commissions, mortgage fees, repairs, maintenance and cleaning, advertising to tenants, insurance, utilities, property management, mortgage interest, legal fees, the cost of replacing broken down appliances, taxes, tax-return preparations, and legal fees. You also ought to factor in the time and the expenses you will cover to get you back and forth the property.

It is close to impossible to know for sure how much of each expense your investment will take. Therefore, as you prepare to make your investment in the rental property business, ensure, first that you gather as much information as you can, both from owners of similar properties, from tenants and real estate agents. Make sure also to make provision for any unforeseen costs.

Commercial Trade Estate

Commercial real estate refers to property that is exclusively used for commercial purposes. It includes property that serves as offices, restaurants, stores, malls, and industrial parks. Businesses and companies typically lease these spaces to maintain flexibility and cost-effectiveness.

The profitability of commercial real estate should surprise you. It is interesting to find out that McDonald's gets the majority of its profits from its property assets and not from food, despite being one of the most popular fast food companies in the world. It owns property in some of the most premier locations in the world.

Some businesses may own the space they use, but the majority has to pay rent and leases for the space they occupy. A lease runs from between one year to 10 years. Large tenants take longer leases while small businesses take relatively shorter leases. A short-term lease allows the owner more flexibility in terms of adjusting the lease rent, but the long-term ones provide security.

Commercial property is categorized into three classes. Class A is made up of property that is rated among the best in terms of age, aesthetics, location and the quality of the structure. Class B buildings are those that are older but are not competitive as class A buildings in terms of their prices. These buildings are sort after by investors who want to flip them. Class C buildings are those that are very old, usually more than 20 years. They are located in the lesser attractive areas and need maintenance.

Investing in commercial real estate can be lucrative and act as a good hedge against the market's volatility. Investors can reap massive profits from appreciation, but the majority of the returns they will get through rental income collected from the tenants.

In most cases, the properties are sold as entire buildings like an office building, a restaurant, or a factory. However, if an investor wants to reap more returns from the deal or hopes to see the profits more quickly, he ought to break down the project into smaller units rather than sell it as a whole.

Flipping Houses

Flipping is a term that was coined in the United States to refer to the practice of purchasing an asset that generates revenue and then quickly reselling it at a profit. As such, flipping houses is the practice of a real estate investor buying houses, then selling them at a profit. When you buy a house with the intention of flipping it, you must be ready and equipped to sell it quickly. The time between the purchase and sale can only be a maximum of one year.

There are two kinds of house flipping:

a) An investor purchases a house that has the potential to increase in value once the structures are repaired and updated. Once the work is done, the investor sells the house for a higher price than was purchased.

b) An investor purchases a property whose value is rising rapidly. Here, no updates are made. The investor only holds the property for some months before reselling it at a higher price, thus making a profit.

House flipping, when done right, is a great investment vehicle because in only a short time and with only small repairs or renovations, you can reap so much more than you paid for it. However, the flip can quickly go the other way. Some people purchase houses and later find that the foundation of the house is shaky or that the roof is leaking. Fixing these issues could cost too much money, or not be worth doing at all, and in the end, you could lose a lot of money.

Ways to Flip Houses with Success

i. *Use cash to finance the house flip.*

House flipping is double-edged; it could succeed or go south. This makes it unreasonable to add to your debt when flipping the houses. If you choose debt, you increase your costs because you will have to pay interests for it for some months, which increases the price to be charged to ensure that the investor breaks even. A highly priced house could take time to sell.

Financing the flip using debt money could cause you to be desperate and act out of desperation because if the house has stayed a while, you may be tempted to lower your prices, which will eat into your profits.

ii. *Study the market.*

Many flippers get excited about their next project and may forget to study the current market performance. Without a clear

19

understanding of the market, you could experience a number of issues. For one, you will not have an idea of whether you are getting a good deal on the house you intend to buy or not. Ideally, you should only buy a property for 80% of its value, then subtract the costs of the repairs.

Without proper market knowledge, it will also be impossible for you to assess the value of the property and its potential value accurately. The vision you have for the home should also fit into the reality of the neighborhood you are buying into, such as their ability to afford the house you are pursuing.

Lastly, without adequate market knowledge, you will have difficulties pricing the house. For example, if the house range in a particular neighborhood is 130k to 150k, you need to work out a plan so that the price you bring to the market after flipping the house is on the lower end of that range.

iii.   *Have a budget for the house you intend to flip.*

Make a budget even before you purchase the home taking in the cost of the property, the repairs, and marketing it.

iv.   *Focus on the smaller renovations.*

Investors have big dreams for their projects, such as hardwood floors, trendy light fixtures, and professional-grade stoves, among others. However, if you focus on doing grand things like these, the budget could quickly get out of hand. A budget beforehand will help to keep track of the updates while ensuring that you up the value of the house.

v.   *Seek the advice of a local expert*

For successful flipping, a real estate agent would be of great help because he will help you identify the right properties, offer advice on the kind of renovations that could lift the face of the property, and help you sell quickly.

Rent, Interest, Tax Benefits, and Appreciation

Regardless of the kind of property you own, the benefits you reap from your ownership of real estate property are in the following forms:

Rent

Rent refers to all forms of payment made to the owner of a townhome, single-family home, commercial building, condo, industrial and crowd-funded real estate. Most people that choose to invest in real estate indicate a preference towards investing in property and leasing it all out to a tenant. Rental income is a source of stability because it is predictable, steady and consistent, especially in a market with a high population because a high demand leads to high rent rates.

Therefore, when you want to invest in property that could bring you income in the form of rent, ensure that you go through the list of local vacancy rates to determine the kind that is most needed by the customers.

Some property owners choose to pocket the entire amount they make through rent payments and then take up all duties that related to the upkeep and maintenance, but other property owners decide to take up the maintenance, upkeep and other services of a property management company in exchange for a small percentage of all rent paid. Drawing from the typical average rates, assume that a property manager will ask for 10% of the gross amount collected, for long-term renters. The commission rate for short-term rentals is much higher.

Interest

The returns that real estate investment companies and private equity firms pursue in their generation of real estate profits generation pursuit are called interest. The details of this method are simple: someone gives the real estate developer or investor a loan to buy property and then collect back the interests and the fees charged, and through this method, he can generate profits.

If you take up this strategy, you take on the role of the bank as the source of funding. This is a legitimate investing strategy for the real estate market.

Tax Benefits

One of the realities of the real estate market that many fail to notice are the tax benefits. When you invest in real estate, you are immediately turned into a nosiness owner, and in this capacity, you are entitled to tax deductions, in the United States at least. These deductions will cut through the costs you incur maintaining and upgrading your property, cleaning and maintenance supplies you purchase, traveling expenses and other costs you bear.

So far, however, depreciation is the most attractive thing about investing in real estate. Depression is the sack of gold coins at the end of the glistening rainbow that the investor collects at the end of each tax year. Simply, the IRS allows investment property owners to depreciate the value of their property over a specified period. To be specific, investors are allowed to devalue their properties every 27 and a half years.

Let's say that you purchase a property for $ 300,000. The IRS will allow a (300,000/27.5) tax loss every year, for 27.5 years, or for the length of time you will hold the property. If you do the math, that's a $10,909 tax loss each year.

There is a catch, however. Besides having to 'recapture' this amount when you sell, the $10k plus tax deduction per year outweighs having to pay back to the IRS a portion, later.

Appreciation

In some real estate markets where the costs of property keep moving upwards, owners of property can earn returns only for purchasing and holding the property. This increase in value is called appreciation, and it translates into profits one the property is sold.

This investment method is suitable for people looking to invest in the long-term particularly in a market where prices are forever moving upwards. Investors in this market should be comfortable with just the long-term-buy-and-hold strategy because even without having to develop the property or do anything else similar to that, the prices are guaranteed to rise and the property will have appreciated.

Are You Suited for Real Estate Investing?

Investing in real estate is trendy, and everyone will want to get in a piece of the action seeing that the value of real estate will most certainly rise. Everyone likes to outsmart the system and make some extra cash. However, the reality is that real estate is not a trade for everyone. Some people will excel at it while others are better off pursuing alternative investment options.

If you want to assess whether real estate is the right investment vehicle for you, consider the following factors:

Do you possess the skills needed for investing in real estate?

Unlike other forms of investment, real estate investing requires that you can make careful considerations, calculation, and monitoring to excel and to keep tabs of the market landscape. If you are going to outsource the services of a property manager, you need to come up with a plan detailing how you are going to deal with them. If you choose to maintain your property yourself, you need to plan on how you will handle the upkeep and maintenance work, and this can be challenging and time-consuming.

Think about the tenants. Some tenants are problematic: some won't pay rent; some will make it unbearable for other tenants while others could damage your property. Ask yourself whether you are able or are ready to handle this before earlier on.

Lastly, ensure that you are motivated, you have adequate knowledge of the market, and that your organizational skills are on point before you make an investment decision.

Market Favorability

Even when you have the right skills, the knowledge and the capital you would need to start investing in real estate, making a move as at now would be wrong. For example, if you are operating in a market that is on a declining trend, on top of a bull market, it will be difficult or impossible for you to profit from investing in real estate.

That is not to say, however, that any time the market is in an unfavorable position you should shy away from making investments. Even in times like these, you can still invest by looking for investment opportunities outside your area and favoring those that are in a much better market climate.

Adequacy of Resources

You should never invest by paying a down payment of money you would not be comfortable losing. Therefore, avoid going all in on investment property if losing the money you have invested would leave you in a dire financial situation were it to fail.

The Commitment

If you intend to lease or rent your property, be ready for the responsibilities and the demands that come with owning property like that. For example, you will need to coordinate cleaning, emptying trash cans, collect rent, conduct repairs, screen the tenants, and various other tasks that you cannot afford to fail.

Note that if you do not have the time or the ability to do any of these things, you have the option of paying someone to assist you in doing it, but this will dig through your income a bit.

Chapter 2: Real Estate Trading

In real estate, trading refers to the practice of acting in place of your consumer. You could buy or sell a property for the customer and earn some amount. Trading also relates to commercial property management and leasing property. In addition, trading is also the arrangement in which you sell a property and buy another simultaneously from the person to whom you are selling. In all of these scenarios, the intention of the broker or the agent is to make some money.

In this chapter, we focus on two of the most profitable yet not-so-popular real estate trading strategies, discussing how they are done, and the perks of each.

Wholesaling Real Estate

Wholesaling real estate is done when a real estate wholesaler places a distressed home under contract with the intention of assigning that home to another buyer. The wholesaler is not concerned with renovating and selling the property. Instead, he intends to market the home to potential buyers at a higher price than what was agreed on in the contract. In the process, the wholesaler makes a profit. The profit is the difference between the price from the contract into which he entered with the seller and the amount that the buyer paid up. The wholesaler's primary goal in this deal is to sell the home before the contract he has with the homeowner elapses.

Let's see what a wholesaling scenario would look like. Suppose a wholesaler gets into a contract for a house at $90,000, and he estimates that it would cost him $20,000 to conduct the repairs and the renovations needed to lift the face of the house. Once the repairs are completed, he expects that the house will sell for $150,000. Looking through his network, however, he finds an eager buyer who is willing to pay $100,000 for the house. Immediately, the wholesaler assigns the contract he had made to the new investor who will then sell it profitably after fixing it a bit. Without even owning the house or doing any reconstructive works on it, the wholesaler will have made $10,000.

The key to avoiding losses and getting stuck in the wholesaling business is to add a contingency clause to the purchase contract. This clause will allow the wholesaler to pull himself from the contract safely if he cannot find a buyer by the time the contract closes. The clause puts boundaries on the risks that the wholesaler can bear.

Wholesaling is similar in form to house flipping; only that the time it takes is quite short, and there are no repairs and renovations performed. In addition, since the wholesaler does not practically buy the home, the business is much less risky compared to flipping.

Wholesaling real estate also involves a significantly smaller amount of capital compared to flipping. The profits are considerably lower, and the money that exchanges hands in the flip is quite lower.

Overall, success in the wholesaling business requires an in-depth knowledge of the real estate market and a good connection to sellers and investors, to enable quick sales.

Properties You Could Wholesale

a. Multifamily properties: Property ranging from small duplexes to large apartment buildings can be wholesaled. Only realize that from 5 family units going up, you will be dealing with a commercial property

b. Single-family homes: This kind of property is the most likely choice for the wholesalers. Units like these are many, and most people understand them.

Townhomes and condos also fall into this category.

c. Land: You could also wholesale parcels of land, whether vacant infill lots or large commercial pieces.

d. Mobile and manufactured homes: Sophisticated investors are again choosing mobile homes. As a seller, you could wholesale them in single units, or as an entire park.

Finding Wholesale Deals

If you are interested in venturing into this viable business, here are a number of places you could look to get the wholesale deals:

Auctions: There are many auctions across the country, and wholesalers can go there to bid and win on wholesale priced deals.

Brokers: Most properties listed publicly often seem a little too overpriced, but real estate brokers may have an idea on some attractive fair priced off-market properties that you can take up. The experience of dealing with a broker will also teach you how to negotiate with a client and how to look out for deals in the market without requiring the help of a dealer again.

Distraught homeowners: Many reasons drive homeowners into a state of worry to the point of wanting to sell their property. They could be having legal troubles, dealing with the disputes of inherited land, going through a divorce or even wishing to relocate fast to move to a different house or area. You can reach out to people in these kinds of situations either using a lead list or through marketing.

REOs: Banks, credit unions, special servicers, mortgage lenders, and even the government can provide helpful information and clues on the location of the real estate property. These institutions will inform you of the property that has been taken back in foreclosure and need to be liquidated.

FSBOs: The "For Sale by Owners" are the properties that are marketed by their respective owners online, but you could also spot their signs if you drive around the neighborhoods

Why You Should Be Venturing into Real Estate Wholesaling

The reasons that make wholesaling an attractive trade include:

- *Needs lesser resources compared to other real estate investment strategies*

  Real estate wholesaling does not require as many resources as other investment paths do. For you to become a property manager, a builder or an agent, you will need some considerable training, licensing and a significant amount of money is need upfront to invest. Buying rental property or rehabbing them requires a lot of money, skills, access to credit and a reliable financial backup as reserves.

As with any other venture in life, having more money and better credit makes things smoother, but this is not necessary with wholesaling. You can engage in wholesaling even without needing your credit score to be checked, and without having to place any significant amount as down payment for your deal.

- *It is a quicker avenue of getting into real estate.*

If you need an easier and faster way to get into the real estate industry and to begin to enjoy the big returns sooner, choose wholesaling. You will not require a license, and you do not need to join a realtor association either. You will not even need a fancy office or even a cheap one, and a college degree is not required either. If the real estate field interests you and you would want to improve your finances like yesterday, wholesaling is an excellent way to start.

- *The business is scalable.*

  One of the important specs of wholesaling is the scalability aspect. This makes it suitable for people on different levels, from those that are only looking for an avenue to supplement their incomes, to those who want to build big businesses and reach their highest career and financial goals.

  Wholesaling generally scales well, rapidly, both up and down. If you need to take a vacation for some weeks or a month, scaling down is easy. If you want to reach a financial goal pretty quickly, then you have the opportunity to scale things up to get the money you require.

- *Does not take much time*

  One of the aspects that cause wholesaling to tower over other real estate investing methods is the amount of time it takes. This is in regard to the time you have to put into the business and the amount of compensation you will receive from doing so.

  A wholesaler is his own boss and will design his own schedule, which means that there are no age limits. Whether you are in the market searching for a job or whether you are retiring from one, you are ripe for the business. You can even get into wholesaling while still juggling your other career, the only thing you need to do is to set aside a little time to wholesale.

The advantage of this job is that as your own boss, you get to determine your off days, your vacations, the amount of travel to make and you can make time for things that matter like spending time with family and catering to their needs.

Once you have immersed yourself into the business, you will be surprised by how much you can make and the amount of time you will be able to dedicate to your personal issues. Your life will be more balanced as opposed to when you held other jobs.

- *The pay is quick.*

  It is easier and quicker to get the money. Majority of the wholesalers are able to turn around their deals in just 3 days. However, even if it takes you as long as 30 days, you will still get paid much earlier than other sources of income would.

The Advantages of Wholesaling

In addition to the perks mentioned above, here are a few more reasons wholesaling is more attractive compared to other investment strategies:

- *The risks are low.*

  If the chances of losing your capital or your property are high, getting into a business of any nature cannot be justified. In this regard, wholesaling foes not offer much risk, to the point of earning the 'no risk strategy' name. However, since it is safer to analyze every aspect of the business, it is wiser to term it as a low-risk venture because it has some of the lowest risk options.

  The small property holding periods (if at all there are any), the minimal use of your capital, the acutely discounted assets, and the multiple exit avenues are a combination of factors that ensure the least risk for wholesalers. This is an excellent get in, get out and get paid strategy.

- *The wholesaler deals with large volumes.*

  Flippers and rehabbers get to work with only a limited volume of property at a time, sometimes only one. If for example, a rehabber is dealing with 4 projects at one time, he may end up dealing in about 12 for the entire year. A landlord who owns many properties is also likely to outsource the services of a real estate management company. However, for a wholesaler, doing 10 deals a month is no big deal. Even if you only do 2, you will be dealing with twice the amount of property the flippers are dealing with. What's more, due to the volume you are dealing with, your earnings will sometimes get to the level that the flippers get—or even more. The good thing is that you will do all this without taking on unnecessary risks and without taking so much time.

- *The profit margins are great.*

   Wholesaling has great returns, and unless you choose otherwise, the overhead costs are low, which creates a large profit margin. When the amount that capital wholesalers earn is determined, their rate of return is almost limitless because it is nearly all profit. You get to choose the amount that you want to make for each deal because there are no limits.

- *Suitable for all markets*

   Wholesaling is suitable for all kinds of markets. You wouldn't want to venture into something that is illegal in some places and unsuitable in others. Some real estate investment ventures may be impractical in some market conditions, both the prosperous and the tough times. It also does not matter where you are located, whether in Las Vegas, new your city, or even in a small town, the rules are the same, and the trade still works.

REITs Investing

Real Estate Investment Trusts (REITs) are a regulated investment vehicle that allows for investors to invest collectively by pooling their funds and investing in the trust with the hopes of earning income and profits from the real estate. They become the beneficiaries of the trust. The money that the investors get comes from rental income, or the money got after the sale of the assets collectively acquired. The returns are then distributed fairly to the shareholders at the end of that particular financial year. Some of the income-producing ventures that the investors have invested and collect rental income include hotels, shopping malls, office buildings, resorts, apartments, and warehouses.

The global real estate market has enjoyed exponential growth over the years even though the costs of financing project development remains high even when the rate of supply in the market is low, especially for housing that targets the lower market segment. The high cost of housing has mainly paralyzed development in this sector. However, to remedy this problem, governments across the world are looking to encourage real estate investing through

REITs where real estate is traded like the stocks and investors can purchase and sell shares as regulated by various marketing authorities.

REITs are avenues for creating money because they enable the concentration of funds for the development and purchases of real estate properties from a number of investors.

With REITs, the REIT trustee acquires the property on behalf of the investor and holds it. The trustee then takes the responsibility of appointing and supervising a manager and of ensuring that the assets of the scheme are invested going by the rules in the Offering Memorandum and the Trustee Deed. The Trustee also ensures that the distributions from the REIT assets are made as is indicated in the Offering Memorandum.

Kinds of REITs

There are three kinds of REITs:

a) Development REITs

Also called Mortgage REITs in some jurisdictions, this type brings together resources with the intention of acquiring eligible real estate property to be used for construction projects and development such as the construction of housing projects and commercial projects. Once the development or construction work is done, D-REITs are converted into I-REITs. When this happens, the investors who purchased the D-

REITs will have the choice to reinvest, sell or lease their shares. They can also convert their shares into I-REITs.

Mortgage REITs are lesser in number compared to Equity REITs. When the REITs lend money to owners of property or buy existing securities that are backed by mortgages, these traits earn income from the interest that accrues from these mortgages. Under a specialized focus, these REITs can also invest in commercial and residential mortgage markets.

b) Income REITs (I-REITs)

Also called Equity REITs, this is the type of REITs that pools together the resources of investors to acquire real estate that will generate income in the long-term, whether residential, commercial or any other kind. I-REIT investors get their returns through rental income and appreciation. The appreciation benefits are distributed among the unitholders at an agreed time.

c) Hybrid REITs

Just as its name suggests, this type is a mix of Mortgage and Equity REITs. It gives investors the advantage by its stability and its income potential courtesy of the interest earned from the mortgage loan.

Tradability of REITs

REITs are also classified according to their tradability. Publicly traded REITs are those that are listed on the stock exchange. You can invest in this kind with just a single share, at a minimum.

Private REITs are those that you can buy, but they are not listed on the stock exchange. Since this type is not publicly traded, the terms of redemption are often set by the Trusts.

Public Non-Listed REITs are those that the public can buy, but they are not listed on the stock exchange. Similarly, their redemption programs are determined by individual companies.

How REITs Work

For companies to qualify to be called real estate investment trusts, they must meet some requirements that Congress set. The conditions are:

- The company must be eligible to be called a corporation going by the IRS revenue code, and not less than five people are allowed to hold 50% of the shares.
- The company must be under the management and direction of a board of directors.
- The company should have been able to derive 75 percent of the income got from real estate transactions.

41

- At least 75% of the income must be coming from real estate.
- 75% of the company's assets must have been invested in real estate, the U.S. Treasuries or held in cash.
- 95% of the income the company has must be passive, such as the rental income.
- The company should be able to pay at least 90 percent of its taxable income as dividends to the shareholders.

A REIT that satisfies the requirements mentioned above is exempt from paying corporate taxes. Therefore, unlike other corporations that pay taxes on what they earn, REITs do not have to pay taxes, and all the money is passed on to the shareholders in the form of dividends. This is the reason some people refer to REITs as pass-through investments. The investors, however, have to pay taxes on the dividends they receive, using the ordinary income tax rates. However, new legislation has recently allowed investors to deduct 20% of the income from the REITs investment, which has lowered the maximum tax rate imposed on REIT dividends to 29.6% from 39.6%.

Kindly note that REITs are not distinct or separate from your normal stock portfolio; they are not a substitute or an alternative either. REITs are a part of that portfolio and work to increase or complement the diversification of your investment portfolio. For your portfolio, you need four different kinds of holdings. You need cash with which to conduct your transactions such as pay your bills and make short-term investments, you need stocks for their returns, you need bonds to provide a floor for when your stock falls, and you also need real estate to reduce the volatility of your investment while increasing possible returns.

Advantages of REITs

Besides the already mentioned benefit of exemption from corporation tax, and income tax, other benefits include:

- *High yields and returns*

The income streams from REITs are predictable because of the long-term lease agreements that holders have with tenants, which makes the management costs and the rental income flow somewhat predictable both in the short-run and in the long-run.

- *Increases access to capital and investments*

  REITs mobilize savings from groups and individuals, which means that the groups and the cooperatives will be able to make substantial investments in the real estate market. This mobilization makes financing easier for people in the middle-class in a manner that does not strain them, as would the capital intensive purchasing of property.

- *Diversifies the investment portfolio*

  Real estate investors have the advantage of choosing from a variety of real estate from investing in industrial projects, residential projects, and others.

- *Investment is managed professionally.*

  REITs provide investors with access to investment professionals like fund managers and property managers who have an in-depth understanding of the market and the industry, and they know how to spot opportunities that others would not.

- *Simple tax treatment*

  Different from other kinds of partnerships, issues of taxation in REITs are forthright. REITs are excepted from stamp duty, VAT, and for taxation purposes, the dividends are allocated to ordinary income, capital gains, and returns on capital. At the corporate level too, REITs do not pay taxes, but the investors are asked to pay individual tax on the dividends at the ordinary income rates. However, the number of returns or capital gains will only be taxed when the REIT sells.

- *Transparency*

  REITs are naturally traded and listed in the public domain making them naturally very transparent. In addition, Trustees and managers are required to occasionally disclose financial information to the investors mentioning the new developments and the risks involved.

- *Liquidity*

  Unlike when you make direct investments in real estate, which are generally illiquid, Income REITs are easily converted into cash by offering them for redemption or selling units of them in the market

Disadvantages of REITs

- The termination of lease agreements, the lack of renewal and the failure to secure new tenants in a timely fashion causes a decrease in rental income.

- Close-ended REITs deny the investor the opportunity to access the investment before the investment period lapses. As such, it becomes impossible for the investor to redeem his investment before the investment period lapses, unless there was a prior arrangement, having secured the consent of the Trustees, to sell the investor's units.

- Changes in taxation affect the returns from REITs. Although REITs are exempt from stamp duty taxes, VAT, and others, this privilege changes depending on who is at the helm of power at a time.

- There is a limited pool of investors for this trade besides the fact that institutional investors are only allowed to invest 30% assets of trustees.

- REITs face stiff competition from other asset classes like stocks and bonds.

- Changes in the political and economic scene affect the value of the property.

Chapter 3: The Different Types of Real Estate Properties

Real estate is possibly the most popular and the oldest of the investment classes. Although many people know that, not many understand the different types of real investment properties, which limits their investment ability, portfolio, and even basic interest. Of course, each of them has its own risks and benefits as you shall see.

Here are some of the real estate property types:

Turnkey Property

The word 'turnkey' is coined from the idea that the real estate property has been made ready for occupation and all that the investor needs to do after purchase is to 'turn the key.' Underneath this loose definition, what exactly is a turnkey property?

47

A turnkey real estate property is an apartment building or home that has been renovated, and an investor can immediately purchase and live in or rent out. This kind of property is traditionally purchased from companies that specialize in the renovation of an old property. Fortunately, these same companies offer property management services to their customer, which significantly reduces the amount of effort and time that the investors have to spend on the property they have purchased.

Turnkey properties became popular during the 2007–2008 recession that came after the housing bubble burst. At the time, buying and owning a home became cheaper than renting in many parts of the country. This investment approach did and still does attract, people who want to be involved in the real estate business but lack the ability or tie to handle the renovation and maintenance issues of a home. In many cases, the investors have hired an independent company to handle the property management processes, but with time, there has emerged real estate companies that offer a complete package, including the maintenance.

How Turnkey Properties Generate Income

Once an investor has purchased a turnkey property, it is expected that it will be available for occupation immediately because the idea behind acquiring real estate that needs little to no refurbishment is to ensure that the property starts to generate revenue immediately. The only work that may remain includes plumbing repairs, replacing electrical fixtures, flooring fixes where necessary and adding a fresh coat of paint to the interior. With only these few changes to make, the sooner the property is ready for rent, the faster the returns on investment will start flowing in.

It does not make sense to renovate a home fully if the intention is to sell it rather than putting it for rent. The expenses that a developer will put into conducting the repairs such as adding a new coat of paint may not be the selling point that buyers are looking for because each comes with his or her own ideas about how the place should look like. This also means that the real estate agent should not be involved in the tearing down or doing away with any refurbishment that the current owner did. After all, the money the agent will spend on the repairs is only likely to increase the asking price of the property. Therefore, the only repairs you should be conducting are only those that will bring the building up to code.

Benefits of Turnkey Properties

The most obvious of the benefits is the fact that there are more properties to consider when buying. If you took the time to study the area in which you live, you would be able to assess the houses that are for sale. Where the number is large, the prices will be low, which means that you can save some significant amount if you have this information beforehand.

Second, turnkey properties are a great source of passive income, which is the entire reason people invest. Owning and being in charge of the management of a property is a full-time job, and purchasing a turnkey property gives you the freedom to step away from all the heavy lifting, and you only focus on ensuring that the property is giving you back your investment. Your earnings should go upwards gradually, only demanding little, if any, effort from you. If you go further and employ a property manager, then you no longer have to care for the property, you only have to wait for the returns.

Third, buying a turnkey property implies that you are buying the specific property for less, which makes the property a better deal, especially because of the income you expect to make from it. If you contract the services of a turnkey real estate company, the company will go ahead and buy the property and clean it up before presenting it to you. Once the sale is complete, leave the property with them. Although they will make money from managing the property, you will be the legal owner.

(A turnkey real estate company is similar in form to a regular real estate company, only that they deal primarily with turnkey investors. They use their expertise and experience to offer investment advice to their customers.)

Risks Behind Turnkey Investing

The risks include:

a) It is risky to entrust your investment to another to manage it.

Although turnkey properties are preferred because the investor does not have to spend too much time on it, this kind of arrangement can be quite risky. You will be leaving the responsibility of assessing the tenants and renting to a company. Giving away your freedom of choice and decision-making can be difficult to do. Therefore, ensure that you scout the market for the best property management company, and then take your hands off, allowing them to take charge from there.

b) The possibility of lacking tenants

Once it is newly released to the market, the property may not have some or all tenants for a while. This is the reason why many turnkey investors advocate for owning more than one house so that when some units are empty, the buildings with more occupied units may support the others. If you only own one house and do not get tenants to occupy it for a while, you will have to bear the burden of absorbing the cost of management and the probable loan you have.

c) The risk of buying unseen

This mainly happens when investors buy property through real estate companies without really seeing it before the refurbishing and assessing its potential. This is risky because it could work both for and against you because you could end up purchasing some property that costs more in terms of maintenance, nibbling away a considerable amount of the profits.

From the assessment, turnkey properties are not ideal for all people. However, if you want to invest in a considerably expensive area, then the turnkey strategy is the way to go because you will use less money than you would be buying the land and then constructing it. It is an ideal investment vehicle for investors that want to invest and gain that extra passive income without having to go over the management process. Therefore, depending on how involved you want to be, choose the proper way to invest in turnkey properties.

Vacation Rental

A vacation rental is a property that is purchased to be used as a second home or a rental property that brings in income to offset the costs of maintenance and to bring a profit. Vacation rental property is best purchased in an area that is popular as a vacation destination so that the property can be rented often.

Ensure that you invest in a location that is frequented by tourists, one that has attractions like casinos, beaches, national parks, lakes or mountains. The place should have adequate and high standard amenities. Recently, vacation rental properties have become a popular alternative for tourists looking for alternative accommodation while on vacation. Most tourists now prefer the home setup instead of living in a hotel and will opt to rent a house for as long as their vacation will last.

Investors can find vacation rentals advertised online, from a turnkey real estate company or with the help of realtor working locally at the vacation destination. Your choice of real estate property should be guided by the popularity of the destination you have chosen, the expected returns on investment, the affordability of the property, the rental market rates in the short-term and the occupancy rate of the hotels and vacation rental properties around. Therefore, in your search, opt for a tourist area that not only has the main attractions in the area but also has an investment advantage.

For example, Las Vegas is famous for its casinos, Orlando is known for Disneyworld, Pensacola is popular due to its location on the coast while Nashville attracts tourists for its music scene. While these cities have some of the best attractions, some like San Francisco and New York are said to be too expensive, and the returns on investment are not adequate.

Always target areas whose local occupancy rates reach 70% and above. This makes an excellent rule of thumb that is useful for when you are deciding on the location to make your investment. You must keep in mind the fact that many of the tourist destinations are seasonal which means that the occupancy rate, among other indicators, will fluctuate.

Rent rates also change in the short-term. Ask yourself if you can afford to pay all your bills even when the tenants are yet to arrive or when the rents fluctuate depending on the tourism season. If you can cover the bills comfortably, you can go ahead and invest in a vacation rental.

You should also consider looking for a vacation rental that makes sense financially. Perform a cost-benefit analysis to ensure that you can afford the apartment even when its occupancy is zero. Consider the vacancy rates of other similar businesses in the area as well as their short-term rates, and compare them to your costs of operation and monthly financing.

Ways to Make Money with Vacation Rental Properties

The most popular ways of making money with this kind of property include renting it out as an Airbnb, VRBQ and for hosting hotel programs.

Airbnb

Airbnb is an online application that allows property owners to rent their vacation property to tourists who are looking for hotel room alternatives. To market the property as an Airbnb, you need to create a profit using a description of the amenities that the guests stand to enjoy. The charges that require payment from you include a 3–5% service charge for every booking. If taxes are relevant to your situation, they should also be added. All costs are then subtracted out of the host's payout.

Hotel Program

This is another money-making option for owners of property like this. Hotel programs are for locations that are already enrolled in a hotel plan such that the investor is allowed to take up the hotel's management services to manage the hotel program by himself. This option is suitable for people who want to rent to their property but want to do it under a strict rental schedule. The rates for these rentals are higher than those of Airbnb because of the hotel services offered.

VRBO

The *Vacation Rental by Owner* is an online branded site where vacation owners advertise their property for tourists visiting the area can see it. Investors manage the property themselves or hire a property manager to take care of business, including that of marketing the site online. This kind of rental is different from the Airbnb because of its different fee structures.

For example, the property owner has to pay $399 as an annual fee for when using long-term rentals, and an 8% booking fee, which is interchangeable with a 13% booking fee if you want the company to manage the property for you. These costs are subtracted automatically from the investor's payout.

Multifamily Home

Investing in a multifamily home that contains two or more units is different from investing in a single family home. You probably will need to take up a loan to facilitate the purchase.

Below are six factors to consider when researching the structure of the neighborhood, and when choosing the lender, in a process that should not take longer than 2 to 3 weeks.

1. Research neighborhoods that would make excellent investment grounds.

You need to decide on a suitable neighborhood even though you will not be living there. Your property should be at a location that is desirable to tenants, so that the units may be occupied as soon as possible. You could first look into the neighborhoods that have multifamily homes up for sale before narrowing down to your home of choice.

In your search, take note of the following factors: the attractions, the amenities, the walk score, rating of schools there, availability of public parking, availability of public transportation, the businesses nearby, the condition of properties around and the overall condition of the area. Conduct this research with the help of a local real estate agent, and then drive around the city to see these things for yourself.

A good rule is to choose a property that is utmost an hour to your desired property's location from where you live because it makes it easier to drive there to meet contractors, inspect the property, and make service calls.

2. Find a lender and get pre-approved.

Once you have found your choice property, get a lender who offers multifamily loans and whose application process is easy. The lender will give you a pre-approval letter which you can submit to the seller to make your offer. Lenders are best sourced online because getting a local lender who specializes in multifamily homes can be quite a task. Check the lender's rates, terms, customer service, areas it covers, and the conditions of the property that it can cover. Your local real estate agent, the bank, or even another investor may also be able to refer you to a lender.

Your choice lender will seek some introductory financial information which is meant to get you pre-approved or pre-qualified. He will then give you a pre-approval letter indicating how much money you qualify for and the interest rates for that amount. The letter will signal to sellers that you are serious and will afford to purchase the property.

The letter should act as a guide for your budget because that may be the only money you get for investment. Factor in the costs you are likely to incur such as the renovation costs, repair costs, carrying costs (insurance, taxes, utilities, mortgage), and the closing costs (title insurance, lender fees, property taxes, and property insurance).

3. Seek an agent's services.

Although you may have laid out facts on the table already, your budget and possible neighborhoods to invest in, you still need to work with a real estate agent, especially one who is knowledgeable about multifamily properties and one who has worked in that neighborhood a while. An agent will help refine the search, arrange for showings and help you negotiate a price.

Choose an agent based on his or her availability, experience (of at least two years) with multifamily properties, location, and specialty.

4. Narrow down the search to a single property.

Once you have thoroughly researched neighborhoods, your pre-approval letter in hand, and an excellent agent by your side, it is time to narrow down the search to the single property you want to purchase. Although your budget and choice of a neighborhood should have already narrowed down the search, it is also important to ensure that the property will have a positive cash-flow now and in the days to come. Also check the condition of the property, the rent roll, the vacancy rate and the expected revenue versus expected expenses to see if it makes sense to invest in that property.

5. Boldly make an offer.

Once you have found the ideal property, make an offer. From this point, the real estate agent carries the load, and to this point, you need some clean deposit money to accompany your pre-approval letter. The offer you make should be subject to your financing and appraisal. This means that if your loan is not approved even after an honest application, you will not lose your deposit. It also means that the property ought to appraise the sales price agreed upon, or you will not make the purchase.

A multifamily property must have more contingencies than would a single-family property because you will need time to conduct your due diligence about the rental history of the property. The due diligence takes about 15 days, and the owners should be able to provide you with the rent roll, costs of maintenance, tenant payment history, and others. Examine these details to help you make a final decision on whether you still want to pursue that offer.

6. Receive the funding and close on the deal.

After making an offer and presented your pre-approval letter, it is time to get the actual funding. This is where your lender gives you a financing commitment. The commitment is stronger than the approval letter because by now, the lender has had more time to look into your details and confirmed the information you provided.

For funding, you will need to provide additional details like the property appraisal, a complete mortgage application, documentation showing the source of the deposit amount, purchase contract, details of the property, rent roll and lease copies, and the application fee if they asked for it. Before you go to the closing, ensure that you get insurance for the property and landlord insurance for yourself.

At the closing, the seller and yourself will sign some documents. The seller will transfer all the security deposits paid to you, and you will receive the keys to your new property.

Apartment Rental

Many people dream of collecting rental income from owning an apartment or a number of them. This idea is especially attractive because, in many cities of the world, rental houses are in short supply while the demand is high, driving the costs up high, all the while, allowing the property owner to reap the benefits. The demand for rental houses is not about to go down because more people want to live closer to where they work, which means that people who own property near downtown or property that has an ease of commute into the workplaces stand to benefit from the attractiveness of their property to the growing workforce, year after year.

Property owners who do not have time to be landlords can hire property management companies to take on this responsibility. The company does this at a cost, which means that the investor has to weigh out the costs of handing over the property management role versus the time and energy he is willing to dedicate to the new business.

If all of the above mentioned has picked your interest, look out for the pros and cons discussed below:

Benefits

- *Apartment buildings are easier to scale.*

  In only one purchase, you get to own multiple housing units, all under the same roof. One transaction could get you to hold 5, 20 or even 100 units. The high number of units might make management somewhat challenging, but the returns are high too. What's impressive is that it will take you an equal amount of time to acquire so many units, as opposed to building a unit at a time.

- *Easier to finance*

  A real estate owner who owns more than five units owns a commercial building, and this makes him eligible for a business loan. Loans like these are easier to obtain compared to residential loans because they are based on investment rather than person liabilities and assets.

- *The benefit of economies of scale*

  The fact that all your investment is under one roof makes maintenance easier and cheaper. If you have a leaking roof, you only have to replace one roof as opposed to what you would do it you owned ten single-family houses, and they all had leaking roofs. You also only need one insurance plan, and you will need the services of one property management firm. Everything is done once, and for the benefit of all housing units.

- *Gives you more control over the value*

  The value of a building is tied to its performance and the revenue the owner receives from it through the collection of rent. Therefore, repositioning the building in an intelligent and savvy way will lead you to enjoy more benefits and in a quick way.

Risks

- *Requires intensive management*

  Typically, property owners experience issues and difficulties when dealing with tenants. Therefore, with a larger number of them living in your apartment rental building, expect that a more significant amount of issues will arise.

Other unforeseen issues arise, which could impact the amount of money you receive as rental income. For example, a tenant could lose his job and not be able to pay rent for some months or a family could split and the partner that remains might not be able to cover the rent by himself. There is also the issue of children who in their adventures come up with a million ways to destroy your property.

Generally, accommodating a community of people in your property is a lot of work.

- *The costs increase.*

  The larger the number of units to be maintained, the higher the costs of maintenance. Think about it: the costs of disposing garbage will increase driven by the frequency and the amount to be disposed of, the water bill will rise, and the amount you have to pay to the property management company will be higher than if you were paying for the maintenance of a single unit.

- *Your attention is still required.*

  You need to know that even if you hire a property manager, your attention and time will still be required to an extent.

- *Cannot be moved quickly in the market*

  In addition, unlike stocks that you can sell readily, this is not the case for an apartment building, and if you do, you will lose handsomely.

- *Requires a lot of reserve money*

  You will need to keep aside a lot of money to cover the repairs and the unexpected vacancies too. Keep in mind that many of the monthly expenses are fixed and do not depend on the occupancy rate. Therefore, these bills have to be paid whether the units are all occupied or not.

Commercial Rental

Commercial real estate is the kind that is leased out specifically for retail and business purposes. Common categories include space for offices, hospitals, retail, industrial, leisure, and even some multi-family housing. Land that has been purchased with the intention of erecting any of the spaces mentioned is also classified under the commercial property category.

It is an undeniable fact that commercial real estate investing is one of the prime gateways towards building incredible passive wealth. This kind of investing has so many advantages over property bought for residential purposes, such as the potential to bring forth a higher income. The cash flow is steadier, leasing contracts made are more attractive, and the risks of vacancies are significantly lower.

However, commercial rentals are not without their own hurdles. These properties require potential investors to conduct due diligence before entering into a purchasing deal. One of the principal requirements is that the investor should research to study how commercial rentals work carefully.

Commercial rentals work this way: an investor purchases a property that is used only for business purposes, then leases the space he has bought to as many business units as the spaces available, and then collects rent from each of them. The businesses could be used for industrial, office, retail, warehousing, and other uses.

The Benefits of Commercial Rental

Investing in this kind of real estate can be rewarding, both financially and personally. Many do it to gain financial security and freedom in the days to come. Others take advantages of the tax benefits the property brings, and the increased diversity in their portfolios that the property brings.

Other advantages include:

Increased cash flow: One distinct advantage of commercial real estate is the ability to bring a consistent stream of income. Typically, commercial properties involve longer leases unlike the residential kind, which means that the rental income is reliable and steady.

In some cases, the tenants are also expected to pay the operating expenses of the commercial property in what is known as a triple net lease. This includes paying the building's insurance, maintenance cost, and taxes besides the monthly rent. This exempts the owner from these payments and increases the profit margin, hence, higher profits.

A higher income: The primary drive behind investing in commercial rentals is the high-income potential of the property. Generally speaking, commercial buildings offer higher returns on investment of about 6 to 12 percent while the single-family properties fetch 1 to 4 percent only.

In addition, the vacancy risk for commercial real estate is lower because the property is spread across different units, and lease agreements cover a longer time than those of residential property.

The competition is minimal: There is less competition in this investment venture because investing in building offices, malls, shopping complexes, and others are outside many investors' comfort zones. Very few are willing to take that risk.

Longer leases: One of the most attractive aspects of commercial real estate is the attractive lease contracts. Commercial buildings have leases that last long periods compared to residential buildings. Most tenants lease properties for many years.

Chapter 4: Passive Income

Real estate has become one of the most famous avenues of making passive income. You may be surprised to know that you do not have to own brick-and-mortar property to get in on the big returns. We already covered wholesaling, and we found that a wholesaler does not even have to buy property to make a decent earning. He only needs to change properties from these hands to the next. Well, there are also other ways that you can make passive income from real estate aside from the apparent method of owning a brick-and-mortar property.

Other ways to make real estate passive income include:

Crowdfunded Investing

69

Crowdfunding is the new and exciting way for real estate investors to pool capital—not by requiring one person to get a massive chunk of the investment, but by pooling a large number of investors each of whom contributes a small amount. The main difference between the traditional methods of pooling money together and crowdfunding is that crowdfunding is done through the Internet.

For example, business owners may turn to social media platforms like Twitter and Facebook to market their ideas directly to a broad audience of would-be investors. This form of raising money has become more popular in comparison to older methods of raising money. Large developers use the crowdfunding platforms to solicit investment funds from accredited investors, while small business owners launch online campaigns to raise funds for their smaller investment ventures.

Types of Crowdfunding

Crowdfunding essentially offers the investors two options. They are:

1) Equity Investment

Many investors take this investment route because it provides better returns than debt investing. Equity investments provide the investors with an ownership stake in commercial and residential properties and turn them into direct owners through their share ownership.

If you choose this investment path, your returns will be directly dependent on the rental income flow less the fees needed to run the crowdfunding platform. If, by chance, the property itself is sold, you will also get a share of the appreciation value. However, normally, investors receive their payouts at the end of every quarter.

Benefits

- There are no limits to the returns you can get. The annual returns sometimes rise by 18 to 20 percent, and investors can even receive more because there are no caps on equity investments.

- Investors enjoy tax benefits. Since you directly own the property through the shares you hold, you can deduct the expenses that you incur through it (repairs, depreciation, and other maintenance) as you calculate your annual income tax.

- The fees you have to pay are considerably low. Instead of having to pay monthly or upfront fees to maintain your shares, you have the option of making your payment annually.

Cons

- It is risky: when payouts are made, you will take second place, and if the property does not make profits, you do not stand to receive any returns.

- The holding period is long: If you desire to increase liquidity in your portfolio, equity investing is probably not the way to go. It has a long holding period that could last anywhere from 5 to 10 years.

2) Debt Investment

Debt investing infers that you, as the investor, are only a lender to the owner of the property. From your investment, you will just get a fixed return based on the interest rate of the mortgage loan that the owner took from the bank and based on the amount of money that you invested. Lenders receive their payments every quarter, or every month depending on the agreement made and since this is debt investing, the owner will give you prioritize your payment during the payout.

Benefits

- There is less risk. With debt investment, there are lesser risks because the property owner is the one who carries and manages the mortgage loan. If he fails to pay the loan, you can recover the amount you invested through a foreclosure action.

- Returns are steady. You have an idea of the returns you will get beforehand, and you can then decide whether to invest or not. The time you will receive your dividends is also predetermined, which makes this a reliable option. The potential of returns falls between 8 and 12 percent.

- The hold time is short. Since debt investment is often made alongside development projects, the holding period is only about 6 to 24 months.

Cons

- Returns are capped. Returns to lenders for debt investments are dependent on the interest rate of the mortgage loan that the investor took, which limits or caps the returns that an investor can get.

- The fees are higher. When you start investing, the crowdfunding platform you are at may take some money off your payout.

The Benefits of Crowdfunding to the Owner

Crowdfunding saves money and time because it takes advantage of the user-friendly platform of raising money for investment.

Using direct marketing for crowdfunding also serves as a marketing tool for your business.

When projects succeed, and the investors are happy, they give positive feedback that markets your property by word of mouth to potential renters. This way, you will have secured both the lenders and the renters, which will secure your business in terms of both the rental income flow and the availability of money for investment.

Crowdfunding adds to the number of possible funding options while enlarging the investor network you can use to grow different real estate projects.

It enables you to gain useful feedback from the online community which you can use to address any flaws, and thereby ensure that your terms are attractive to the lenders and that the tenants get what they are looking for.

REITs

REITs, already discussed in a previous chapter, are an excellent source of passive income from real estate investing. A REITs takes the form of a mutual fund because it carries within itself different types of investments within each investment package. However, for a REIT, all investments within it must be from the real estate field. For example, a REIT will give you ownership of different kinds of investment, from warehouses, office buildings, shopping malls, healthcare centers to timberlands. REITs can house many more types of real estate property.

Investing in only one real estate investment such as in a rental home can be risky because anything can happen to jeopardize the stability of your income and your property. Therefore, ensuring variety in real estate investment will mean lesser risks for you as an investor because your eggs will not all be in the same basket.

REITs are either non-traded, exchange-traded or private.

a) Exchange-traded REITs

Exchange-traded REITs can be purchased from a broker, and they are registered through the Securities Exchange Commission, the SEC. Their owners are also required to file reports with the SEC occasionally. You will also find the exchange-traded REITs with various national security exchanges such as the NYSE and the Nasdaq.

The one major downside of the exchange-traded REIT, however, is that its performance mimics the performance of the exchange it is listed on, just like an index fund mimics the performance of the index. For example, assume that a REIT is listed on the NYSE. If the NYSE performs well, the REIT will perform well, and if the NYSE plummets, the REIT follows suit.

b) Non-traded REITs

Non-traded REITs work a little differently from the exchange-traded REITs although both of them are listed with the SEC. The non-traded REIT is also expected to file reports with the SEC occasionally. However, these kinds of REITs are not traded publicly and are not listed on an exchange. This denies the non-traded REIT liquidity as an asset. However, both kinds are indeed sources of passive income drawn from investing in real estate.

c) Private REITs

This is the third REITs option. Private REITs are not listed on the SEC and therefore are not required to file any reports with the body. However, this lack of connection with the SEC makes them riskier investment ventures compared to the other two.

Traditionally Owning Real Estate Property

Investors are not one to forget the old ways of doing things. They take up the traditional method of owning real estate properly because when it is done the right way, it can be a source of passive income. When you are deciding to invest in real estate property as a source of income, you have the option of either choosing to invest in commercial rentals or residential rentals. This does not eliminate the fact that there are also other kinds of property that you could rent out like farmland and timberland and reap some returns.

If you choose to go the traditional way, make arrangements to have someone manage the property for you because if you fail to do so, you will have tenants ringing your phone every minute to ask questions about the house, to notify you of areas that need repairs and many other issues that are likely to arise.

You need to stay on your toes and ensure that you conduct all the maintenance work on the property. You will also have to go through the tenant applications and to do background checks for all applicants. The collection and deposit of rent will also be your responsibility.

If the tasks mentioned are a bit too much for you, you will find it necessary to hire a property management company as mentioned severally before. The company should work on your behalf to ensure that everything is running smoothly. Only check to see the amount that your company of choice charges so that the fees do not eat into your profits too much.

Land

Land, in its raw form, can be subdivided and split. If you perceive that some land is located in an area that is likely to grow and progress, then you ought to buy it up and wait for the surrounding area to be developed before selling it for a hefty profit. The advantage of this type of investment is that there will be no tenants to deal with while the downside is that if the property is not desirable in any way, do not expect the land to appreciate, hence there will be no cash flowing in.

Owning Mobile Home Parks

This is becoming a popular real estate investment style these days. This type of investment is known to do quite well during hard economic times when people cannot afford to purchase homes, or even pay their rent, besides other utility bills. Mobile homes become the choice form of housing, but the people need to be at a particular location for their safety, among other reasons.

Owning the piece of land on which these mobile homes are placed places you at an advantage of receiving rent from the homeowners.

The advantage of this method of earning is that the tenant turnover is very low especially if your property is safe and in proximity amenities that the people need. The downside is that it is very difficult to secure a loan for this purpose and even if you succeed, the project tends to be capital intensive.

Industrial Property

This is a lesser exciting real estate investment vehicle, but it brings in money, which is the primary focus of any investment plan. A property owner offers up his property to businesses to use the space for warehousing or manufacturing. The advantage of owning this kind of property is that the returns are high and steady, and the management required around the property is minimal if any.

The downside, however, is that the property houses typically only one tenant which means that in case the tenant vacates, it is rarely easy to find a replacement, and the property may sit unoccupied for a long time.

Individual Storage Facilities

These days, it is not just the businesses and the companies that need space to store their goods; individuals also hoard more and more stuff, and they need enough storage facilities to take in all the items. The advantage of owning property like this is that the owner does not have to deal with everyday tenant problems as he would in a multi-family living unit. There are no overflowing toilets or rude and loud tenants to deal with. There will not be a tenant that died on overdose and the authorities coming for you to record a statement.

The downside, however, is that the investor becomes very reliant on property management companies who can either make or break your business mainly due to their quality of customer service.

Airbnb

Some people have figured out how to make money off their unused rooms in their primary residences or at the vacation homes they own by renting the property out through Airbnb. The advantage of this is that you get to make more for each night than you would make if you rented the space out for the long-term.

The downside, however, is that you have to continually worry about the people you let on to your property and have to worry too, about the length of their stays. However, this constant worrying can be mitigated by having a property management company handle issues for you.

Tax Liens

The government expects all homeowners to pay their taxes, and if they do not, the government will place a lien on their property. A lien is a legal claim for taxes owed on the particular real estate property. The government then auctions off these liens, and savvy investors fight to get a hold of them. In this way, the investors can acquire property that are on ridiculously low prices.

The upside of making this investment is the potential to make huge gains, while the downside is that understanding exactly how to invest in tax liens takes considerable knowledge and experience.

Chapter 5: How to Turn Real Estate into a Long-Term Business

Name some of the wealthiest people you know or have heard of, and I bet you that 80% of your number, if not more than that, have made their wealth through real estate. These investors didn't start by owning many properties. They started small, with only one— and their businesses grew, taking on a third, a fourth, and so on. Many people say that real estate is one of the most significant vehicles to financial freedom, and indeed, the numbers are a confirmation.

Owning real estate property is not just a great way to build your long-term wealth—it is also one of the best ways to diversify your portfolio. The primary reason that human beings build long-term wealth and diversify their investments is to have something to lean on in their old age or something to fall back to when one type of business is not doing well or when it collapses.

When you want to go ahead and make a step towards investing, start by answering the following critical questions:

1. What do you find more exciting and more fulfilling than residential and commercial real estate?
2. How much money do you have for investing at your disposal?
3. Are you looking to make the investments using your own money, or will you use other people's money? In case you opt to seek investors, is debt investing the way to go, or will you give them a share of your business?
4. Is the investment or the business you are trying to build intended to be a part-time hobby, or are you looking to make it a full-time business? Could it also be a part-time interest that you hope will morph into a long-term business?

The above questions are essential to help you determine where you are headed with your investment efforts. The third question is particularly crucial because debt is what will ensure your speed in business. With a vast capital resource, you will be able to grab opportunities as they come and to make substantial investments that attract consumers more than the small investments, among other things. Money makes the entire investment process easier, more efficient, and therefore, more successful.

Once you have answered each of the questions above, you can now move on and begin your ascent following the steps and the advice below:

1. *Embrace the Humble Start*

If you haven't made any real estate investments in the past, do not jump ship with all your valuables. Avoid using all the resources you have—even if you can afford to do so. Not one of the successful real estate investors will tell you about how the first investment they made propelled them to greatness. You are still green in the business, and you need to learn the ropes of it. For example, you are yet to know how to read and interpret contracts—you still haven't built your network of real estate professionals, and you are yet to develop a right eye for the business. All this knowledge comes from experience and not from a textbook.

The beauty of the business is that you will have the opportunity to learn all the knowledge you would need just by the small deals. For example, you could try finding cheap properties—say, a single-family home, multi-units, or a commercial property—and use them to practice the trade by presenting them to customers and negotiating with them. Ensure that for the first several deals, you only commit very little as you get to learn the ropes of the trade.

If you do not have money to start buying property, do not let that slow you down—you can still do wholesaling. Wholesaling allows you to enter into a contract for a particular property, putting only very little money down, even less than $1000. You should then work hard to move the property before the contract expires. Best-case scenario, you will make between 5 and 15 grand that you can reinvest in other long-term holdings. Worst-case scenario, say you did not put any contingencies; you will only have lost a grand.

2. Go Big

The real estate business can be overwhelming sometimes, and it is easy to give up especially when you haven't got any money. However, the money ought not to scare you, the deals that you get into are the ones that matter. Therefore, as you turn your interest into a long-term business, ensure that you are pursuing the deal and not the money.

Someone was talking about a real estate investor who saved up $50,000 and then started chasing deals worth $200,000. The fact is that with that amount budgeted, you cannot pursue more than 4 units, and each of the units can only bring you $1,000 and $2,000 each month. What's more, you can only get this money after using thousands of dollars in renovations to make the units rentable. From this analysis, this money is just not enough.

For this reason, you must go big right from the start. Let's say that you take up a minimum of 16 units. Don't be tempted to take less than 16. Now, with 16 units, you can now take on the services of a manager, or you can now take the opportunity you now have to direct all your attention towards the property.

Managing 16 units, you will need to wait and save some more money or pool other people's money. However, you will learn how to ask people for money, and you will learn how to sell.

3. Understand the Market, and Get a Mentor

In real estate, the choicest of the deals are the ones that are easiest to find like purchasing property that has management and a tenant in place. However, these properties will give you some of the lowest returns. However, the property and the deals that will provide you with the highest profits are those that other people do not know about, which you will find without any hustles.

For example, the best time to go about flipping houses is when the economy is strong, inventory levels are low, consumer confidence is high, and the interest rates are extremely low.

The low-interest rates allow the retail buyers to purchase a home rather than what they would have purchased when they are afraid of debt increasing under medium level and high-interest rates. The strong economy and high consumer confidence give the consumers the feeling that the right time to buy property is now. The low supply also called low inventory creates a high demand, which in turn causes investors to bid against each other, raising the property prices and allowing the investors to make

85

more from the sale.

Therefore, if you can secure a property before the competition begins, then you will be able to transform your small initial investment into considerable returns in only a short period, particularly if you are flipping homes.

In case you are looking to make tax-advantaged passive income, the rise of the sharing economy through services like HomeAway and Airbnb have created short-term renting, which is no producing some of the highest returns on investment. You can even get 20% returns on good property that is located in areas with many attractions.

It is unfortunate, however, that there are still pitfalls in real estate. Therefore, you will need to educate yourself on some of the pitfalls that investors fall into, and how you can avoid them too. Source this knowledge from online sources but keep off the books, articles, and how-to videos because they contain little information especially in areas that investors should be wariest of. A mentor is also important because he will offer you advice based on the personal successes and failures he has had. He will also teach you some of the tricks he has acquired over the years, those that he uses to maneuver the market to get the best deals.

4. Prioritize Learning Against Earning

Yes, you have worked hard to earn that money, but before you spend it all on the 60-inch large curved smart TV you have been salivating over, consider spending that money educating yourself. Seminars and coaches are not a learning platform either. However, no matter how much they insist that you need an expensive education, you really do not. There is information everywhere, and the more substantial proportion of it is inexpensive; get it from someone who is an expert in real estate.

The way to grow your wealth in real estate is to build wealth by holding property. Having a shelter is one of the basic needs, which means that someone will come asking to rent your house for a specified period. As you purchase land in or around the metropolis areas, remember that land is a finite resource. If you cannot erect buildings at that particular time, someone else will. Therefore, if you own prime land, one of the immediate responses is to try and construct something. That rental will help you pay back the mortgage you took when purchasing your land. As you pay off your loan, choose to rent and to hold for something bigger,

In your investment, ensure that you do not spend beyond your budget. Most real estate projects you invest in will have surprises and overruns in them, but this is just the nature of the business. Therefore, keep aside some amount to cushion you against the unexpected. Levering your funds also help to lower risks and increase returns. What you do, you ought to start with one project, and then slowly graduate to the second. Continue making progress, and soon your real estate portfolio will be solid.

The most important lessons in real estate include the need to continually learn, hustle and aim for value addition or creation. Ensure that you take massive, ambitious courses of action every day. You also ought to speak to contractors and brokers every time you can; accompany them to meet-ups, or to view houses and on your way, learn something new. When you are ready to invest, knock the doors and ask to buy the property. The best deals are the ones where the owner is not prepared to sell. Find that property and then find someone to buy it, and you will have earned money on your first deal.

5. Make Your Mark Immediately

In real estate, there are three primary strategies you need to take note of:

The first is that you ought to purchase low-income property to start building your portfolio. Let's say you have bought a house for between $35,000 and $50,000. The costs of purchasing this property will be low, but you should expect consistent yields. On doing that, hand over the property to a property manager and start earning rental income passively. Assume that the returns will be of between 8% and 10%.

Suppose you buy two or three more properties like this every year, in 10 years, you will have a portfolio of 20 or 30 houses, each giving you an amount I rental income. Already, you will have turned real estate into a long-term business.

The second strategy is that if you can do the repairs and fixing yourself, you ought to consider a 'live-in flip.' In this strategy, you begin by purchasing a house that only requires a little work on it for a great deal and lives on the property for about a year or two while you renovate the house. Once you are done, move out and flip the house for a higher value than you bought it, and you will earn a profit. Suppose you do this for five houses in 10 years, your earnings from these houses will fall in the $300,000 to $500,000 range net profits. This amount is enough to allow you to build or buy your own house or reinvest it into an apartment or commercial rentals that will cover your cost of living for the rest of your life.

The third strategy is to engage other people in a joint venture in a deal. Most people have the money or know where they can get it; they need some motivation and convincing that they are taking up the right opportunity. Therefore, to get them to give you the money, find an excellent deal and tie up that property with a contractual clause, pending finance approval for 30 days. In the meantime, find an investor to join forces with you in the flip. Explain to them that you have already secured the property on contract and that you only need the funds for a predetermined period, after which you will return the money and split the returns with him. So long as the deal looks reliable, you might be able to get almost anyone on board.

If only you make the right calls, you will easily find an investor with whom you can partner. Only ensure that you have correctly calculated the costs of the repairs and have estimated the expected sale price accurately. If you underestimate the costs of refurbishing the house and overestimate the price of the property in the market, the reality of things will chew into your returns, and you could lose credibility in the market.

6. The Returns Are in the Purchase

Many real estate investors think that the money lies in flipping which they commonly refer to as 'fixer-upper.' However, this is wrong because the money you pay for the property is what determines your profit margin once you sell. Therefore, the real money is in the purchase. Simply put, you make money when you buy the property, and not when you sell.

To ensure that you are buying right, compare the potential value of the property with that of three other similar sales, often called 'combs.' The combs that provide the best estimate are those of the same size, location and value as the property you are planning on purchasing.

That is not enough though; you need to ask yourself

some critical questions. The first is, what would be the realistic sale price for the property after the rehabbing is complete? Secondly, in total, what is the scope of the work needed to attain this value? Do not allow your taste and preferences to cause you to push this value very high up.

Purchasing real estate property offers some core benefits such as it takes a short time to finish conducting the repairs and that the investor can reap some of the most significant profit margins while the cost of purchase is kept low and the price you paid to acquire the property is also very low.

However, before you actually embark on a project, ensure that you solidify both team A and team B. Team A is made up of experienced persons such as fellow investors, your mentor and your financial manager who will offer advice on the risks you can afford to take and those you should stay away from. Team B is made up of the associates who get you going including fellow investors, your mentor and your family.

Once you have built a solid plan, move along with your project. Avoid having backup plans because they keep you second-guessing yourself and prevent you from giving your best to what you are doing. However, ensure that you have many exit strategies to keep you from losing because even the most airtight plan may be flawed. Experienced investors say that real estate investment winds shift rapidly, and the worst thing you would want to have is to be stuck with a dozen unsellable properties.

Lastly, you ought to understand the difference between holding, buying, and trading. Buying you already know but this is no issue because the issue lies in what you do with what you have purchased. However, ensure that you hold on to commercial property for the long-term, but trade residential property as soon as you can.

7. Keep Time

For you to optimize the capital gains, you receive from your investment, and timing must be done properly. Real estate investors often use 12 p.m. and 6 p.m. metaphorically to indicate times that the market is at the peak and on the floor, respectively. Everyone wants to buy when the economy is doing well which pushes the prices upwards, but everyone sells when the market is at the bottom of the cycle.

The problem is that no one can accurately predict whether the market is resting precisely at 6 p.m. This makes the next best time to buy to be at 7 p.m. when the market starts moving up again slowly. Watch the market and coin your trend along the market trend so that you know when you buy and when you sell.

8. Your Intuition Matters

When you are investing in anything, not just for real estate investments, do your homework in depth using all the analytics and the data you can find. Once you have done that, listen to your intuition, your gut feeling. Let both the data and your intuition lead you. Most investors say that some of the best deals they made were after careful consideration and carefully listening to their instincts.

Chapter 6: Tips to Get Financing

Many people fail to understand that their lack of financing does not disqualify them from getting in on real estate investing. You do not require as much money as you have been made to believe, and even for the finances you may need, there are many different ways to secure financing. You only need to take up the right financing method—one that will satisfy your investment goals and aspirations.

Here are some of the investment tips you should take up to secure financing for your investments:

1. Ensure That You Are Not in Debt

If you are only now entering into the real estate business, ensure that you have cleared any prior debts—whether they be medical bills or student loans. You have to clear all kinds of debts before you can start anew. Go ahead and calculate your debt-to-income ratio (DTI) by dividing the periodic debt that you have to pay up by the gross income you receive, on a per month basis.

The numbers you get here will help you and the bank determine whether you can survive to pay the debt as part of your monthly bills. If the DTI is high, then this is a clear sign that your debts are too high and that it would be difficult for you to juggle through them. In a case like this, the bank will even refuse to grant you funds for your real estate purchase. The highest DTI that can receive a mortgage loan is 43%, but it is safer to ensure that the number is considerably lower than that.

2. Start Saving for the Down Payment Earlier On

The down payment is a big deal in real estate because it is how you secure a contract. A commercial real estate property requires a more substantial down payment than personal residential property. The down payment for most investment properties are at least 20 percent of the principal amount, and this does not compare to the 3 percent for residential property.

Suppose you even raise 25%, 5% above the required minimum—you will qualify for even better terms with regards to the interest rate.

In the event that you cannot raise the down payment money, perhaps you can get a second mortgage. However, this is likely to be very difficult to secure.

Therefore, if you are planning to secure a traditional loan, you need to start saving up to make enough for the down payment. You should also remember that a good down payment saves you from the effects of the interest rate because you will not have to borrow as much money. The lesser you borrow, the lesser the interest you pay.

3. Opt for a Fixed-Rate Mortgage

Banks offer a number of financing options, and an investor will have to choose the mortgage plan that best suits his financial situation. You can choose to either take up an adjustable rate mortgage or a fixed rate mortgage.

An adjustable rate mortgage may seem attractive because its starting rate is quite tempting. However, its interest rates will keep rising and falling throughout the term of the loan. However, the fixed rate mortgage is the better option because the interest rate will be the same throughout the loan period, which will help you with the planning because you will know the status of your numbers in real time.

Experienced real estate investors warn against an adjustable rate mortgage saying that the last thing an investor wants is an unstable interest rate because it messes up the investor's cash flow.

4. Keep Your Paperwork Organized

On the go, always have all the important documentation you may need to ensure that all the processes you need to go through are smooth and quick, particularly the routine papers moneylenders always ask for. You also need to have with you proofs of your financial ability through certification of employment and bank statements.

Freelancers need certification from a CPA in addition to a ton of other paperwork depending on your financial and work situation. Some lenders will ask you for your divorce papers if you have gone through one, others will ask for documents to show your legal status and others will ask for financial reports to show financial activity outside your credit report.

Therefore, organize all your documentation well and be prepared to fish them out when requested for them so that the investment process goes on as smoothly as possible.

5. Have a Clean Credit Profile

The first thing that your lender will check once you walk into the bank and make your funding request is to check your credit score. The credit score is the first determinant of whether you qualify for a loan. To be granted a low-interest mortgage, your credit score should be high. Generally, a credit score that is less than 740 will only get you a high interest while a higher one gives you the privilege of qualifying for a low-interest mortgage loan.

Therefore, if you are interested in taking a mortgage in the future, keep an eye on your credit scores. Avoid delaying your obliged payments and if there are errors in your payment trends, have it fixed immediately.

6. Realize That You Will Pay for More Than Just the Value of the Property You Are Buying

Besides paying the agreed upon value of the property, realize that you will also be paying for other expenses and you may not have any more money at the time. Therefore, you need to budget for these expenses too in your loan negotiation. Estimate what it will cost you to cover the maintenance costs, the operating costs, and the running costs. You also need to factor in even the unexpected, unforeseen expenses.

7. Be Creative in Your Approach

If you are trying to secure a property that has a high chance of increasing your profits, consider making your down payments or accessing your renovation money using an equity line of equity using credit cards or a life insurance policy.

For the actual property purchase, you may be able to secure financing through personal loans got from peer-to-peer lending sites that connect individual lenders and investors. Only prepare yourself mentally that you will face a lot of criticism and skepticism about the deal especially if you have not dealt with too many real estate properties. Some of these crowdfunding platforms also make it a requirement that your credit score as an investor meets particular criteria.

Realize also that if you choose to borrow the money from a single person as opposed to an organization, the lender may be very conservative and protective of their money and will be wary of giving their money to a stranger.

8. Request for Owner Financing

In the past, requests for owner financing was a reason to rouse the seller's suspicion of the potential buyer, but this was only during the days when not many people qualified for a bank loan. However, with the tightening of credit, you can now request for owner financing. However, if you choose to go this route, have a precise game plan.

For example, you could say, "I would like to pursue owner financing for this amount of money and under the following terms." Convince the owner about both you and the idea of financing your project.

9. Keep Off the Big Banks

If the amount you have secured for the down payment is not as much as it ought to be or that you have other mitigating issues opt for a neighborhood bank instead of a large national lender. This is because the chances that you will be financed here are higher than if you make your application at a large financial institution that considers issues raised from all parts of the country.

The local bank will be more flexible, and they may also have a better grasp of the local real estate market and have an interest in helping local investors.

Mortgage brokers are also a great funding option because the brokers offer a fuller range of loan products. However, conduct adequate research before you settle on any of them.

When it comes to real estate, do not expect that what worked for others will automatically work for you. Do your research by looking through different financing methods and then compare them before you make a decision. Be realistic and pick the financial strategy that you would be okay with and those that will propel you towards reaching your real estate investment goals I the long-term.

Methods of Financing Your Real Estate Investments

There are many financing options available for all kinds of investors, but unfortunately, not many people can take up these financing options. First people are afraid because real estate is capital intensive and they are afraid that if they take up loans, the properties may not sell or the rental income may not flow in as expected. However, if you look through the loan list, you can identify a loan whose terms will appeal to you and suddenly make the road to real estate investing not so scary.

Home-Style Renovation Loan

This type of loan is Fannie Mae-backed, and it is primarily issued to investors to finance their primary residences that may have one to four living units. However, these loans are also available to investors who are looking to flip a second single-unit home or an investment property.

Investors who are looking for investment for more than one unit of investment property should look for financing elsewhere. In addition, the home-style renovation loans are exclusively permanent mortgages, which means that investors looking for short-term loans cannot benefit. Therefore, this kind of loan is best suited or investors who are buying and renovating a single-unit property, and then holding it.

Fix-and-Flip Loans

The fix-and-flip loan is a short-term hard money loan that investors seek for purchasing, renovation and selling of investment property. A typical loan of this kind has a lifespan of between one and three years although the investors who flip property typically use the loan to purchase and fix up property that they hope to sell in 3 to 12 months. Fix-and-flip loans are usually divided into rehab loans and purchase-only loans.

Investors seek the purchase-only loans to finance the purchasing of property that does not need renovation like when the investor wants to season a property or do something similar before refinancing to make it a permanent mortgage later. On the other hand, investors use rehab loans are used to finance the purchase and renovation of a property before it is sold or to refinance it to become a permanent loan.

Blanket Mortgages

A blanket mortgage is an exclusive kind of mortgage because it covers and finances different types of properties all under one mortgage. Because of this, investors can use the same mortgage to purchase two or more properties as a single investment. However, commonly, lenders only approve blanket mortgages for investors who are dealing with five or more properties under one loan.

There are no restrictions on the types of properties that the lender can finance under this loan type. While it is only required that the properties be in good condition before the financing is done, there are no restrictions in regards to the number of units to be financed. As such, an investor can seek funding for several multi-unit properties using only one loan.

Typically, investors who are seeking a blanket mortgage use it in either of two ways. In the first, the investor intends to purchase multiple new properties with only one down payment. In the second, the investor can choose to refinance his multiple existing properties using only one loan.

Cash-Out Refinance

Cash-out refinance is a phenomenon that happens when the real estate investor is making an effort to unlock the equity of an existing investment property to buy a new property. Cash out refinance, therefore, is the act of taking out a new mortgage on an existing property then paying off any liens before he pockets what remains in cash. The cash that he pockets becomes the down payment on the new property—or if it is enough, it can be used to purchase a new property in cash.

The primary advantage of a cash-out refinance is that there are no restrictions regarding what to do with the cash that the investor pockets. This means that the money can be used to invest in any other kind of investment property—without having to answer any questions.

The disadvantage, however, is that the investor will need at least 30% stake on the existing property's equity for the cash out refinancing process to be initiated. This is because the lenders only deal with a cash-out refinancing of between 65 and 80 percent of the appraised value of the property.

Apartment and Multi-Family Loans

Multi-family loans work in the same way as apartment loans. They are mortgages that are used to finance the purchase of residential investment property that has a minimum of five units. The difference is that apartment loans typically cannot finance property with less than five housing units.

The combination of apartment and multifamily loans also offers real estate investors different ways to finance a property with very many units. Therefore, any investor looking to invest in a multi-unit property should look to either of these loans.

The downside is that these kinds of loans can only finance a property that has a small amount of commercially zoned space. However, the loans are not suitable for investors looking to invest in mixed utility property.

Chapter 7: Understanding Property Valuation and Guidelines to Decide You Are Selecting the Right Property

Property Valuation

Many property owners are not bothered or even aware of the benefits of property valuation even though it is right at the core of acquisition and management of a property. Valuation helps to unravel any secrets and mysteries surrounding the ownership of a property over the different kinds of property ownership.

To an investor, an expert valuer is an important asset because he can take note of and advice the investor on possible grey areas in regard to the ownership of the property in question.

A valuer has undergone the training and has the skills he needs to scrutinize different kinds and natures of property deeds. He checks the information indicated in the body of the paper and compares it with the property title. He then advises the client in issues related to various mutation forms and adjacent property values. He also studies and offers his opinion regarding the value of the adjacent property before turning again to interpret survey maps and registry locations.

With the current craze surrounding the ownership of property and creating a long-term business using real estate, many people are rushing to purchase investment properties. Many run the risks of landing on property that is overpriced. However, when they seek the services of a valuer, investors will be able to understand the capital appreciations of the properties that they intend to purchase and own. The information you get will be used to negotiate a fairer asking price.

Through valuation, an investor will be able to tell whether the property or the land that he or she is holding is worth investing in. Valuation also becomes one of the bases of taking a bank loan, as the bank will demand some security against the amount that has been borrowed. The investor can provide unchallenged property valuation to banks, mortgage institutions, insurance companies, prospective buyers, and investors.

Once you get a hold of the valuation report, you will appreciate the details the valuation covers. Beyond containing the details of the property in question, the report goes ahead to report on property trends in the area, factors that affect the price of land, and elements that could lower the value of the property. The report also outlines the kind of property it is, the expected sale value after a long time, and the likely value appreciation to expect over time.

Other details to expect include the property age, the size of the rooms and their layout, any wear-and-tear and the effect it has on the value of the property, and even an assessment on the kind of fittings that were used during construction.

For the valuation process to be fair, the valuer must compare your property with similar others in your area. As such, the value he assigns to your house will be similar to the general house prices in the area. The demand for property in the area, the neighborhood desirability and the location in relation to the amenities that are closest will all also affect your valuation.

The data that the Land Registry has may also affect the value you are given. The government updates house prices in an area monthly in an attempt to keep abreast with the changing property prices in the country, and this too can be a determinant of the value of the house in question.

Therefore, whenever you want to sell a house or even purchase one, the agency you are selling to or the agency that is funding you sends a valuer to have a look and to check what the house is worth. Therefore, if you are selling a property, ensure that the property is in tip-top shape. It should be clean, tidy and there should not be any clutter in and around it. The agent will then move room by room assessing the size and condition of each. The state of the floor also matters significantly in the valuation process.

Why You Should Understand the Valuation Process

The first reason is that once you understand the factors that influence the value of a property, you will be able to take note of aspects of the property that you can use to bargain and to avoid overpaying for your property.

The second reason is that knowing the valuation process will help you ensure that you get a favorable valuation on your existing and new properties. This is because if you can provide the valuer with information regarding the relevant evidence he may be looking for, you will be able to make a stronger case for and influence a higher valuation.

Thirdly, when you understand what the valuer is looking for and you continuously point out the positive traits of your property, that may not be obvious to the valuer. This pointing out is likely to work in your favor.

You must remember, however, that the valuers have worked in their fields for a while and have become experts at evaluating the property. You may not want to appear like you are patronizing them. However, if you are in possession of information that could save both parties some time, many valuers may be open to listening to you.

The Valuation

Using the information that the valuer has collected from the inspection process and by comparing the target property to others that have been sold recently and have similar properties, the valuer will come up with what is called a valuation.

The more the similarities between the current property and the three used for comparison, the more likely that the valuation will be accurate. The properties used for comparison must have been sold recently—at least within the last six months. However, depending on the market trends and how quickly these changes are occurring, the valuers might opt to rely on the sales that have been performed within the last 3 months only.

Once the analysis process is completed, the valuer then compiles a report to outline the properties he used for comparison and evaluates how different the properties are from the current one.

The valuer presents the valuation report to the individual or the institution that ordered the valuation. If the valuation was commission by the lender in regard to a particular loan application, the borrower does not get to see the report, although he can request the lender to provide the valuation figure.

How to Know That You Are Selecting the Right Property

A real estate property is one of the solid assets because it has the potential to grow your wealth tremendously in the long run. However, you can only reap this benefit if you invest in the right property because if you make a mistake in this area, the ripple effects of it will affect you in other areas besides the finances.

For example, it could lead to untold worry, stress, and heartache, which is nothing close to what successfully investing should be about. To prevent you from going through the painful process, here is a guideline to help you stay on the marked path so that you end up with the right property.

1) Know people and talk with them.

One of the most important assets in life are the people; you need them and their input in almost everything you do. Therefore, as you enter the market, the first thing you should do is talk to them, particularly the group of other local investors, because it is from them that you will get to know the market. They have dealt with it first hand and may have a word or two that could enlighten or caution you.

See how you can arrange meet-ups, or link up through the local real estate associations. People often underestimate the value of a network, but it is this network that will offer you guidance and insight that is tailored to your area and the property, you are covering.

2) Determine the amount you would wish to borrow.

Get in touch with a lender to determine the loan amount you qualify for and its interest rate. This is called understandings your borrowing position, and you should do it before you select the property you are going to invest in. This way, before you get excited about a listing and then suffer through the loss when you realize that you cannot make the payment, you will know where you lie.

It also ensures that you only make investments that you can afford. Taking out a mortgage and another one after that will only force you to continually produce substantial payments that will deplete your monthly capital resources. You also start the investment process knowing what your monthly payments are, instead of making the commitment to pay and finding out later that the payments are now higher than you anticipated.

3) Visualize the ideal renter.

Envision the type of people who will be renting your property, and think of the things, including the neighborhood, that would interest your renters. Therefore, you need to find a property that will fit the character of the renters and their ideal neighborhood. You do not want to rent them dingy studio apartments in the middle of an upmarket suburban neighborhood.

For example, if your target market is the young working professionals, you need to purchase property that would be appropriate for their profiles and the area. You will find it easier to fill your units when you make these considerations, carefully.

4) Avoid doing more than is necessary.

Many investors want the property they purchase to reflect who they are in terms of class and preferences. However, fixing a real estate property should only be done for the aesthetics, to lift the face of the property. For example, you can focus on the paint and only work on the hardwood floors and the tiles in areas that deserve the change. Otherwise, if you bury yourself doing major work like the electrical, or the piping because they will considerably shrink your profit margin.

If the house you are set on purchasing has a higher monthly payment than you can raise, try house hacking. This is where you live in the said property for about a year perhaps by living in one-half of the house and finding roommates. When you do this, you will qualify for FHA mortgages and non-investor interest rates.

The added benefit is that when you live in this property, you will learn a lot from it, including how best to maintain it.

5) Estimate the amount you will be earning from rent.

Once you have spotted an ideal investment property, you now need to learn all you can about it. One of the first things to think about is the amount of rental income you can draw from it. If tenants are living in it already, ask the current owner to show you records of its rental history. Compare the rates therein with those of other property in the area to ensure that the owner is honest.

If the owner previously occupied the property and you would want to rent it, check the amounts charged for renting property similar in size, location, and amenities on Craigslist. Learning how much these properties are renting will give you an idea of how to price yours.

While browsing through Craigslist, beware of property listings that have terminologies like 'credit checks are not required' or 'first month free' because these terms suggest that the landlords in the area are struggling to get people to rent in these spaces.

6) Count all your expenses.

Generally, about half, 50%, of all rental income goes into covering the expenses, without counting the loan payments. Therefore, if you require your tenants $1000 in rent, assume that $500 is going towards expenses. Let's say you have three tenants and your loan payments are $1000 per month, your cash flow per month will be$500 which translates to $6,000 per year.

If you want your calculations to be more specific, you will need to include utility bills like water and garbage disposal. You need to count in also the maintenance costs, which will vary depending on the location. Count in even the significant expenses like the roof, the foundation, and the HVAC system (it is easier to ask about their condition before making the purchase).

Estimate that the vacancy rate will take up at least one month's rent in a year. Alternatively, you can also Google the vacancy rates in the area to make the calculation more dependable. Taxes and insurance payments are also a crucial addition to your expenses. Lastly, take into consideration the property management, which should be at least 10 percent of your monthly rent collection.

7) Think about your property's appreciation.

When it comes to real estate, property appreciates either by the forces of the market or by force. If you purchase a house and conduct some repairs that add its value, the house has appreciated by force. On the other hand, if the neighborhood improves in terms of value and amenities, then the market has caused the appreciation.

As a new investor, your focus should not be on forcing appreciation because, in the first place, it would be nearly impossible to estimate the cost-benefit analysis of the repairs you will see through. This is also the reason why flipping is not ideal for new investors.

Market appreciation is easier to understand because you have to look through history to follow trends. However, investors are warned against buying property just because it has an appreciation potential because the winds of investment could change in an instant. Instead, look for a property that can generate cash flow whether the property appreciates or not.

8) Determine your choice property's cash-on-cash return rate.

This one will require you to do some calculations.

Assume, for example, that you have invested $200,000 in rental property, inclusive of the down payment and all the closing costs. Say this investment earns you $24,000 each year that makes the cash-on-cash return a whopping 12 percent.

Anything above 10 percent is to be celebrated, although the returns are also reliant on the market. To determine the property that would give you a good cash-on-cash return, you will need to crunch the numbers for many properties.

New investors are asked to consider at least 30 to 50 deals before they can finally make their pick. When you do this, you will start to notice that the lower and upper bounds begin to distinguish themselves. With time, as you get to know more and gain interest on a property, you will know where it lies (the bounds are already defined).

Investors are, however, warned that they should not get so caught up in determining the cash-on-cash returns that they forget to look at equally important issues like the condition of the house. In addition, investors don't have to find the ideal and maximum possible cash-in-cash return; they only have to find something that lies in the top 25 percent but one that is also in an excellent condition.

9) Evaluate your rate of capitalization.

The capitalization rate is the amount of time it would take to recover your investment.

If for example, you invest $80,000 buying some

property and you earn $ 4,000 out of it in a year after subtracting the expenses, your capitalization (cap) rate is 5 percent. Therefore, it will take you at least 20 years to recover your initial investment.

Bottom Line

While choosing to invest in real estate is a real temptation, it is not the golden ticket to wealth. The business can be tedious and unpredictable, and you are not even guaranteed to have revenues after investing.

For example, if you have invested $100,000 and if you are getting $1000 in returns less the expenses, you would be better off investing in the stock market.

Therefore, be very careful when investing in property—don't skimp on the research before you dip your toes.

Chapter 8: Tips to Decide a Good and Bad Deal

The process of buying or selling a house is so exciting—there is the thrill of hunting, the pride and self-esteem that builds as you turn down houses that do not meet your standards, and the excitement of having found the right fit.

This entire process becomes even more fun if you have with you an experienced and knowledgeable real estate agent who is familiar with the area and knows the ins and outs of the local market. The able agent will ensure that your property sells at the highest possible price or that you buy your choice property at the best price possible.

However, once you have settled your eyes on a property, it is normal and expected that you might start wondering whether you have made the right decision. Many first-time investors are more likely to worry.

Having observed that, here are three primary things you should know about finding the right property fit.

a. An ethical real estate agent ought not to pressure you into purchasing a house.

b. When you find the right property, you will know it in your heart instinctively.

c. You may think of going ahead to sleep on the idea so that you can make the decision the next day, but this is WRONG!

The idea of sleeping on it has been traditionally known to help people make the right decision—but not in this case. In real estate, everything is wrong with sleeping on it. Why? It's because the business is about trusting yourself and not second-guessing your instincts. It is unlikely that your intuition will lead you in the wrong direction.

There is an old phrase that says, "Shuffle your feet; lose your seat," and another from an old cartoon *Ed, Edd, and Eddy*, where Edd would tell his friends, "You snooze; you lose."

Remember that you are not the only investor scouting the market and seeing value in the property you saw. He will pull the property right from under as you busy yourself counting sheep.

The last thing you would want to hear your agent say is that another buyer has already made an offer and that you missed him by minutes as he walked to make an offer. His offer, which is way higher than yours, was then accepted immediately. This stings too much, but don't feel too bad if it happens to you—human beings are prone to making mistakes.

Therefore, unless you intend on purchasing a newly constructed home, you will not find another home right around the corner similar to the one you just lost. Therefore, when you find the right house, make a move immediately.

How You Know That You Have Found the Right House

1) You have an urge to go inside.

When you pull up to the curb, it is likely that you are excited that this next property could be the one you have been looking for. You look at the house on the left and the other on the right, and you are more fascinated by the house on the left. If from looking at the houses by the curb makes you like the house on the left better than the one on the right, this could be a sign that something about the house on the left has appealed to you. This, real estate agents call curb appeal.

2) You feel embraced the minute you walk in.

In about three seconds of entering into a house, you can tell whether the house is comforting and warm, or otherwise. Does the house speak to your person? Do you feel the urge to explore further? Does the house feel like home? If it does, it probably is.

3) Being in the bathroom does not give you an odd feeling.

Sometimes, investors will feel so uncomfortable when they walk up to the bathroom that they cannot enter it. They are even afraid to let their shoes get into contact with the bathroom floor. Instead, they prefer to stay outside and supporting themselves with the door frame, poke their heads inside for a second.

On the contrary, if you can walk into the bathroom, stroke the vanity marble and open the door to the shower, then this house would be a perfect fit.

4) You begin to visualize how you will arrange your furniture.

If you walk into the living room and can already envision where you would place your TV or into the master bedroom and can already figure out the wall to which you will set your bed against, then this is more likely your house. If you already see where your kitchen items could go, you are captivated already.

5) You see yourself painting your ideal color on the walls.

It is likely that the only thing you do not like about the hose is the deep blue color or the purple walls in the bedroom and you start thinking about how much brighter the house would look with some more brilliant colors. Perhaps orange and white would work. Once you find that you are continually thinking about the house and how you would customize it if you were to purchase it, then go ahead and do it.

6) Your basic needs are met.

The dynamics of the house might not meet every need you are on your list, but at least the basic ones are all met. For example, the house could have all the rooms and spaces you were looking to have; it could be located close to the amenities you find most important like a good school for your kids. However, the house could fail to have a garage, and in a flash, you realize that a garage would not be as important because you can always erect some shade for your car. You could also build a garage once you settle in. Therefore, in your evaluation of the properties, be flexible about your requirements and define which issues would be deal breakers and which ones you would compromise on.

7) You feel that you no longer want to look at other properties.

All other properties you have seen, even those that impressed you a little now no longer appeal to you and they lose their significance in comparison to the property you currently have. In addition, the house you previously thought were somewhat impressive fall so far behind on their rating and look pale in comparison to what you have found. You get the sense that you would feel like a traitor to this home if you went and visited others you haven't seen. If indeed you think this way, the bond has already been formed, and this is it.

8) You are on the edge of your seat, waiting to tell others about what you found.

Once you have fallen in love with the property, it would be so uncharacteristic if you failed to take a few photos of the place and sent them to your friends on various social media platforms after the tour. You will be so excited, and this feeling is bound to manifest itself to others. Before you know it, you are sending every nitty-gritty bit of the house and telling your friends how impressed you were. You even start urging them to come up with a date when you can all visit the property together.

9) Every thought that comes to your mind convinces you further that you need to do something about the house.

While it is impossible to eliminate the small, stubborn, and nagging thought that makes you want to sleep on the idea of purchasing the property, every other thought directs to how this property is an ideal fit for you. You become consumed and cannot focus on anything else. You cannot eat, you cannot sleep, all you want is the new house. Then, by all means, get it.

How to Be Sure That It Indeed Is a Good Deal

While every inch in your body is bubbling with excitement because you have found a house you like, it is also important to ensure that you are getting a good deal so that you do not regret once the excitement starts to die down.

The condition and the location are two critical factors that determine whether a home is a good purchase. Although the price is also a significant factor, finding a property that can be renovated with only a little effort and time is close to impossible. Anyone who bought and fixed up a house knows that there will be hidden challenges and problems that come up without warning, and these challenges are not easy to identify, even with a thorough inspection.

Therefore, the ability to discern with only a single glance the value of the home requires a keen eye. Here are a few tips you can take up to help you scan some of the most critical areas to determine if they are in good condition.

Let the 1% rule guide you.

This rule is used to evaluate the expected returns from an investment property. This is one of the rules of thumb in real estate investment. The rule states that the rental income to be collected every month should at least get to 1% of the investment money for it to have a positive cash flow. The due diligent thing to do is to analyze the rents rates in the area before the purchase because what you charge for rent will be around the same figure too.

Take note of any liens and zoning issues.

In a general manner, one of the ways to tell if you are getting a good deal is when a property has a complication or characteristic that leads to a direct 'no' from many investors. Liens and zoning issues for small properties can be a sweet spot. They are too expensive to be taken up by retail individuals, but they do not provide enough room for institutions.

Assess the capitalization rate.

The cap rate is calculated by determining the price /earnings ratio. Compare the figure you get with the neighborhood, and this should tell you whether the deal is good. Kindly note that some sellers will be more motivated than others which will drive the price upwards, but for a legitimate reason. You could also use the price per door or the price per square foot and compare this to the prices of properties in the neighborhood. Lastly, successive drops in the price also signal an excellent opportunity to buy property.

Get rid of the HGTV hype.

For you to get a good deal on the property, you need to suppress and completely takeout your HGTV hype. Set aside the lofty expectations too. You can still make and save money if you purchase the 'worst' property in the neighborhood and renovate it slowly as your budget will allow. Having old appliances and Formica will not kill you either. A lot can be said about the value of a property over and above the perceived value which is determined by something as minor and replaceable as the kitchen cabinets and the countertops.

Check the condition and the presentation of a location.

The condition and presentation of property are often a telling sign of whether you can get the property at a discount. Therefore, if you cannot seem to find any online photos of the place, then it is likely that the property has zero or negative curb appeal. It also indicates to you that the seller can allow a significant discount on the purchase price and that the property does not have any impressive features. This could only be a quick sale, and you should take advantage of that.

Check the condition of the roofline.

Checking the condition of the roofline is one of the tricks valuers, and property inspectors have up their sleeves. It is the first thing they look at. The roofline only will tell you the interior condition of the house: whether it is complicated, elegant, weak, simple, sturdy or vulnerable. Also check to see if the roofline is original, or whether it has been added onto the property. Does it drain properly?

See if the price is less or more than the monthly rent multiplied 100 times.

If you purchase a property at $1,000,000 and can charge rent of about $10,000 or more per month, then this is likely a good deal. This determination simplifies all real estate investing factors because multiplying the rent by 100 is easy, quick and a significant determinant of a great price on real estate property.

Weigh out the purchase price versus the county appraisal value.

An experienced real estate investor can tell you if the property you are to see is a good deal only by looking it up on the county appraisal district website and checking its address. If you key in the address and you find that the price offered is way below the county's assessed value, the chance of profiting from the property is 90%. You will reap a profit because the fair market value goes with the county assessment value, and you can add about 10% to 20% to the appraisal value. Make this your first step in evaluating the price of the property.

Moving Forward to Make or Accept an Offer

Once you have spent months on end looking for a house and finally have settled on a great deal, what will stand between you and getting the property for yourself is sending the right offer. For both sides of the transaction, whether buyer or seller, the purchase offer is the first step towards finalizing the deal. Both parties have to make their final offer without offending each other so that you can reach an agreement and start taking steps towards closing.

Recently, the real estate market has had buyers competing with each other for the limited number of the available property, which has changed the face of property negotiations. Buyers now have to make offers putting in mind what other buyers are willing to offer.

On the receiving end, sellers must be able to weigh the offers the buyers make carefully, be as transparent as possible and negotiate the terms patiently to keep the deal from falling through later on. Since the winds of the real estate market work in a cycle, the sellers should be ready to see changes that could turn the ball to the other side, and put the buyers at an advantage, over the sellers.

To help you come up with the right offer for the property, to understand what the other side is doing, follow the following steps provided for making, and accepting offers on properties.

How to Put Up an Offer on a Property

Making an offer is not just about mentioning a price to the seller; you also need to prove that you can provide proof of your ability to raise that amount. You also need to indicate the date of your expected closing date and determine how you will cover additional expenses. The seller also needs to indicate what he expects of the seller up until the closing. When you do all this, also be prepared to provide money earnestly, which will indicate your seriousness in taking up the offer. You could give an amount ranging from $500 up to about 10% of the price you agreed upon.

Be careful not to get ahead of yourself though. Only make an offer on a property you have affirmatively determined that you can afford. Your budget should guide you. Once you have done that, the next steps will be much easier especially if you have with you a good real estate agent to help you through.

If you are wondering when to submit an offer, especially if you are looking to buy property in a place where the number of available properties is lesser than the number of buyers, make an offer as soon as possible. Remember when we said that if you snooze you will lose? Make the offer as soon as you feel connected to the property. Even then, you may find yourself competing with other buyers.

To answer the question of the amount to offer, although the listing price should give you a clue about what the seller expects, the work that needs to be done and the property valuation should play a bigger role in determining the amount to submit.

Your real estate agent will sit you down and let you in on the sale history of properties in that area, and depending on those figures, and you can come up with an approximate value of the property. Besides that, you also need to factor in your own needs. For example, think about how the details of the house check off for you and the amount of work you have to do to fine-tune it to your taste.

You need to factor in also details like the amenities in the neighborhood, renovations needed, proximity to schools, work, and stores, the age of the appliances and systems like the plumbing, electric, HVAC and the roofing. Any deferred maintenance will need to be considered too.

It is also crucial for you to attach any contingencies you may need to the offer. Once you are past the price determination and have agreed on it with the seller, there are also some other conditions you need to set to make sure that you are protected as a buyer. For example, if you already own a home and are looking to sell it so that you can afford the new house, you should offer a contingency on the sale of your house if you deem it necessary.

Many sellers like to stay away from contingency offers like that especially in a market where buyers do not have the same constraints. Some buyers may not have cash problems and could be ready to close the deal immediately, which will put your seller at a disadvantage if he settles for you yet you have a contingency. To resolve this issue, real estate agents advice the investors looking for houses to put their current homes on the market before they begin searching for another house. Once you have the new house under contract, you can make the offer using the home-close contingency. This contingency will assure the seller that you already found a buyer for your home and you are only waiting on your closing for your sale to be completed.

Concerning your competition with other buyers, you are likely to be afraid of bidding wars and the reality of having to raise your offer to get the house. However, besides the price, getting the house may take more strategic moves, and establishing a personal touch with the seller.

Here are a number of things you can do to make your offer stand out. Write the seller a personal letter, which works if you particularly realize that the seller has a sentimental attachment to the property. Even if your offer is not the strongest, the letter will tag on to the seller's heartstrings. Secondly, use quirky numbers to catch the seller's attention. For example, instead of $400,000, write $411,325. The second amount will register a higher number, and it will stick to the seller's memory better than the rest.

Lastly, be flexible and willing to meet the needs of the seller. If the seller is looking to move out soon, ensure that you can raise the amount needed by the time the seller is ready to ship move. Sooner closing date will entice the seller.

Accepting Offers

If you are on the seller side, the first thing after putting up your property in the market is to wait for interested buyers to show up. As long as your property is fairly priced in comparison to similar property in your area, buyers will show interest.

Secondly, you need to place a deadline on your offer. A deadline is important because it helps spike interest among buyers. It is also to your advantage because you can arrange for some time to be available for the showing or to let your agent have your keys when you are away at work. Ensure that the deadline is placed only a few days away so that buyers have less time to compare your property with those of other sellers.

Thirdly, understand your limits. As you determine the price to set on your property, have a discussion with your realtor that a buyer would have with his agent. Determine the value of your home based on its condition, the value of other similar properties, and the amount you are looking to get to pay off your mortgage or even purchase another property. Expect that most offers will be below your asking price and determine how much lower you would be willing to go.

You also need to determine basic details like you are expected closing date and the maintenance you need to do before the sale. Making decisions like those early enough will keep you from making decisions driven by emotions rather than logic.

Fourth, you have to sort through the offers to find the best. While the offer price is undoubtedly a primary determinant, you also have to consider other expenses and costs, the financial security of the buyer and whether the timeline stated in the offer would work for you.

For example, the buyer could offer you $500,000 for your house but ask you to cover all closing costs, which could be somewhere between $5,000 and $25,000 and this amount you have to less from the principal amount. You also have to factor in your realtor fees, which could get to another $30,000.

If you value sentimentality, ensure that it does not drive you towards making the wrong decision. Remember also that the law prohibits discrimination against people based on their sex, race, religion, color, disability, the nation of origin and the status of their families. If it is discovered that you turned down a buyer based on these variables, you could easily be sued.

The fifth step is to negotiate. The fact that you have found an offer that works for you does not mean that you have to accept all the terms that the buyer laid in the original submission. You need to negotiate, be it by coming up with a counteroffer for the price, adjusting the suggested closing date, or the modifications and repairs the buyer requested. In the negotiation, you need to be wary of offending the buyer even if you have the upper hand because this could soil your reputation and drag you back to the first step after you have come quite a long distance.

Lastly, when you are ready to accept an offer, enter into a contract with the buyer and begin the due diligence process. Both parties need to sign an agreement that they agree to all the conditions of the deal including the price, closing date and other particulars stated in the contract.

Chapter 9: Common Mistakes Made by Real Estate Investors

Whatever you do in real estate—whether you flip houses, wholesale, own properties or experiment occasionally—real estate investment is quite appealing particularly when the real estate market is strong. However, just like anything else in life, there is a right way and a wrong way to do it.

Here are some mistakes investors make in real estate:

Having a Get-Rich-Quick Mentality

Part of the reason why real estate investing is so popular is that the idea of quick, effortless wealth has been sold to the masses. People now get into it thinking that investing in it is a sure bet that they will make easy and quick tons of money.

The truth is that real estate is just an excellent long-term investment, similar to mutual funds, which is even easier. Most people who talk about the huge returns of real estate purposely avoid mentioning the hard work that goes into it. As you enter the real estate field, keep in mind that you have to be smart and hardworking and that you need to have a considerable ability to tolerate risk.

135

Hurrying to Enter into Deals

Although we have stated that you have to move fast when you come across a property that speaks to you, you need to do this very cautiously. When you are new to real estate, particularly, you have to be patient and take your time to study the market before entering into any deal. Real estate offers many thrills and excitement, but rushing into a purchase can get you into immeasurable problems that will significantly affect your prospects of turning real estate into your long-term hustle.

Therefore, take as much time as you can to study the market conditions—especially along the lines of resale values, rents, and neighborhoods—and review hundreds of sales that have been made before deciding to be part of it as well.

Underestimating the Cost of Renovations

This is a mistake that you will frequently observe among your peers, and you may fall into it as well. Many investors underestimate the amount that it will take them to carry out the renovation ideas they intend to carry out after acquiring the property. Therefore, as you make these estimates, do it in due diligence by getting several quotations from contractors that have carried out similar renovation projects. Once you do that, stick to it, and hold the contractor accountable for implementing the budget to the letter. Any other changes you may desire will have to wait until later.

Failing to Have the Right Community Around You

One of the keys to succeeding in any field is to build the right team. In this case, you need a team of professionals, including a valuer, a realtor, a home inspector, a lender, and a closing attorney. This team will help you with your issues and help your buyers too.

For the renovation and maintenance business, your team will include a plumber, an electrician a painter, a roofer, a flooring installer, a cleaning service, a heating, and air-conditioning contractor and an all-around repairperson. Even if you prefer DIYs, you will barely make any money as an investor doing all the maintenance and repairs. Get people to do that and focus on linking buyers to properties.

Failing to Do Your Homework

A person does not qualify to operate on others and give them medication without going through rigorous training and education. However, some wannabe investors think that they can get into the business and succeed without perusing a book, at least. You must educate yourself before you put your hard-earned money into jeopardy. Therefore, take time to read as much as you can get about the field. Cover as many topics as you can, including information about screening the tenants and buying foreclosures.

If formal learning is not your thing, look for a

successful investor who owns many properties, from residential to commercial properties, and offers to pay for one or two hours of his or her time to learn more about the trade.

Avoiding Due Diligence

Investors have understood the importance of moving quickly in this business. Experienced investors rush to close in on deals, but this is where the newbies trip. They forget to do their due diligence on the deal in regards to the current mortgage rates, maintenance costs, and the market conditions among other expenses, and to cover the overhead costs, they end up taking money out of their personal savings because they cannot sell the house or it needs more repairs and renovations than they anticipated.

It is not unusual to find newbies purchasing property just because they sense that the market is going to appreciate. If you ask for supporting evidence, the investor will likely not have any to support his theory.

Lack of a Backup Plan

Many people purchase property and get stuck with it because they only have one way out. They believe that they can only sell or rent it out, nothing else. It is possible for the rental market to stall, and the property may not even sell as predicted. However, you should have at least two ways to get out of the deal.

For example, if the first plan is to renovate the house, place it on the market and resell it, the alternative plan should be to offer it to a buyer on a lease-purchase arrangement. A third plan might be to hold the house rent it out to derive rental income. You could also have a fourth plan like the option to wholesale by selling to another investor at a price below the market price. Hopefully, with all these methods at your disposal, you will strike a profit. However, the idea is to cut all the holding costs you could incur holding the property.

Paying Too Much Money

This is a common mistake among investors. Many of them pay too much for the properties they want to acquire, which thins their profits. Once you buy the property, realize that you have already locked down the benefits because as we have established, your selling price will very likely be along the confines of the market price. Therefore, if you pay too much, you may be surprised that you will not make any money considering that you will also carry out renovations later.

Planning On-the-Go

Many new investors get into the business without a plan. All they want to do is secure property, and when they have, they have no idea what to do with it. That is working backward, and lack of a plan sets you up for failure.

You need to have a plan even before you start securing property, then find a property that fits into your plan. Don't start trying to come up with a plan long after you have found the house. The problem is that people view real estate as a compilation of transactions rather than as a path towards long-term investment. Most people fall for the beauty of a property, but what matters is not the property but the motivated seller. Nice properties will always be built as architecture develops. Don't let beauty hold you back.

Once you have determined what you are willing to pay on your next property deal, stick to that number and don't go beyond that. To avoid getting stuck at a single property, make many offers on different properties. Stick to the numbers and don't be concerned about the deal you get. As long as the numbers are in your favor, you are good to go.

Failure to Consider Soft Costs

Many new investors do not factor in the soft costs in their analysis of deals. They forget to include agent fees, closing costs and carrying costs for the days they will be holding the property in the market. These overlooked costs often offer a valuable but rather harsh learning opportunity.

Take Investment to Be Speculation

If you are purchasing property with the intention of waiting for appreciation and other market changes to drive the price of the property upwards, you are speculating and not investing. It is okay, and even profitable to speculate. However, you need to know the difference.

An actual real estate investment should be able to offer risk-adjustable returns from the first day when you purchase them. Therefore, don't excuse a poor investment decision saying that you are speculating.

Forgetting That It Is the People Who Are Most Important

Many investors get caught up in the business and forget that the people are most important. Their primary concern is the numbers and the particulars of an area, but they forget that it is the people that are going to buy the property. It is your association with the people that will bring you money. Therefore, as you invest, ensure that you are driven by the interests of the people rather than the money. It is said that if you do business out of passion, the desire to help people access affordable housing, the money will follow. In addition, success in real estate directly depends on the long-term relationship you build with others.

Borrowing from Friends and Family

Investors who are new to the business may come across a seemingly excellent investment opportunity but fail to have the money they need to secure it. Most times, many of them turn to their family and friends to secure funding because this appears to be the best and the easiest way to secure financing for the new property deal. However, this is not a good investment move. Instead, go to lenders, advisors, and seller-financing.

Failure to Use a Good Local Broker

By working with a capable real estate broker, you can rule out the fear and anxiety that you have at the thought of making a mistake or falling for the wrong property. An agent will also protect you from your desire to flip houses prematurely before you have any relevant real estate experience.

He or she will have you understand all possible exit strategies related to your investment and keep you from sourcing projects that are costly and would have you paying steep penalties. Lastly, a real estate agent will have you keeping records of all your activities and expenses to ensure that you stay within the limits of your budget.

Throwing in the Towel

One critical issue that many young real estate investors have is that they get into the business without keeping in mind how difficult the business can get. Although the investor will get many opportunities to make large amounts of money and achieve financial freedom, there is nothing about the process itself that is easy. Like any other venture, there will be regulation or legal issues, people issues, and financial issues. These issues have to be dealt with as conventional businesses deal with theirs.

Conclusion

Thank you for making it through to the end of *Real Estate Investing: Latest Rental Property, Wholesaling, Development, Flipping, and Marketing Strategies*! Let's hope it was informative and able to provide you with all of the tools you need to achieve your goals—whatever they may be.

From reading this book, you have undoubtedly added to your pot of knowledge regarding real estate investment. You have unmasked many myths we hear about this field, and fundamentally, you have realized that real estate is a business like any other.

Real estate is not just about making quick cash as we have commonly believed—we often assume that people who own or deal with many properties are rich, but this may not be the case all the time. Real estate investing is like investing in any other business—it requires a lot of hard work and determination. The money you get is as a result of getting the right property, using the team you have acquired to make changes to the property at minimal cost, using your community to mobilize buyers, and eventually selling to the right buyer. Real estate largely depends on the relationships that you create, and it is by no means a solo project or career.

The beauty of real estate also lies in its flexibility. Investors can get into it as a one-time gig, but they can also use it to build their lifetime business and wealth. As such, real estate is a source of quick money, but it can also be used to ensure financial freedom and security. While this field does not discriminate against anyone by seeking certification or anything like it, getting into it without the right knowledge could lead to tremendous losses. Because of this, this book is the fountain of knowledge that you need to arm yourself and others around you with information on how to reap the best returns from real estate investing.

Finally, if you found this book useful in any way, a review on Amazon is always appreciated!